Lucius E. Chittenden, L. E. (Lucius Eugene) Chittenden

An Unknown Heroine

An Historical Episode of the War Between the States

Lucius E. Chittenden, L. E. (Lucius Eugene) Chittenden

An Unknown Heroine
An Historical Episode of the War Between the States

ISBN/EAN: 9783337191252

Printed in Europe, USA, Canada, Australia, Japan

Cover: Foto ©ninafisch / pixelio.de

More available books at **www.hansebooks.com**

AN UNKNOWN HEROINE

AN HISTORICAL EPISODE OF THE WAR BETWEEN THE STATES

BY

L. E. CHITTENDEN

Author of "Personal Recollections, 1840–1890," etc.

NEW YORK
RICHMOND, CROSCUP & CO.
1893

AS A SLIGHT
RECOGNITION OF HIS HOSPITALITY
AND OF
HIS ASSISTANCE IN VERIFYING THE NOBLE EXAMPLE OF
ONE OF HIS NEIGHBORS,

I Dedicate this Volume
TO
MAJOR DAINGERFIELD LEWIS,
OF AUDLEY,
NEAR BERRYVILLE, VIRGINIA.

THE AUTHOR.

CONTENTS.

CHAPTER	PAGE
I.—INTRODUCTORY,	7
II.—THE VALLEY OF VIRGINIA,	11
III.—A HOME IN VERMONT BEFORE THE WAR,	25
IV.—THE TRUMPET-CALL OF WAR IN THE GREEN MOUNTAINS,	32
V.—THE CALL TO ARMS IN THE VALLEY,	38
VI.—HOW A BRAVE MAN MET THE HEAVY STROKE OF MERCILESS WAR,	42
VII.—DESERTED,	52
VIII.—THE UNCONSCIOUS HEROINE,	65
IX.—THE CONSULTATION—THE COUNTRY DOCTOR—THE DECISION OF THE HEROINE,	76
X.—THE FIRST EXPEDITION TO HARPER'S FERRY,	85
XI.—THE PECULIARITIES OF THE COUNTRY DOCTOR—THE REMOVAL AND CONCEALMENT UNDER DIFFICULTIES OF A STALWART ENEMY,	96
XII.—THE DREAM WHICH WAS NOT ALL A DREAM,	105
XIII.—THE BATTLE OF OPEQUAN OR WINCHESTER—THE PROGRESS OF THE WOUNDED OFFICER—THE SKILL AND ENTERPRISE OF HIS HOSTESS,	116
XIV.—THE BATTLE-FIELDS OF WINCHESTER—THE SEARCH FOR A FORGOTTEN GRAVE—AN ACT TO BE HONORED BY BRAVE SOLDIERS AND EMULATED BY TRUE WOMEN,	126

CHAPTER	PAGE
XV.—A Side View of the Battle of Cedar Creek, with "Sheridan Twenty Miles Away,"	134
XVI.—The Terrible Harvest of War—The Preparation for the Escape of the Wounded Officer,	153
XVII.—The Escape,	165
XVIII.—Rest and Preparation for the Search,	181
XIX.—A Time of New Trouble and Anxiety,	195
XX.—The Afflictions of the Mule-Owner—Preparations for the Search for a Prisoner of War—The Separation of the Friends,	210
XXI.—In the Den of the Ogre, the Terrible Secretary,	223
XXII.—The First Failure in the Search,	233
XXIII.—The Bloody Angle—The Prisoner and His Betrayer,	241
XXIV.—"What I did for Him I Thought Some Northern Woman Might do for my Husband,"	253
XXV.—And the Recompense of a Man's Hands shall be Rendered unto Him,	263
XXVI.—"I have not Found so Great Faith; no, not in Israel,"	272
XXVII.—The Hard Lot of a Prisoner of War—One of Them Touches the End of His Sufferings,	286
XXVIII.—"Weeping may Endure for a Night, but Joy Cometh in the Morning,"	301

ILLUSTRATIONS.

Portrait of Mrs. Van Metre, . *Frontispiece*
Portrait of Major Bedell, ... *Page* 129
Map of Shenandoah Valley, ... " 147

AN UNKNOWN HEROINE.

CHAPTER I.

INTRODUCTORY.

WHILE this volume does not aspire to the dignity of history, the somewhat hackneyed title of a story founded on fact cannot properly be applied to it. It is substantially a true story. Every character in it existed, the essential facts stated, occurred in the order here given. Truth has spun from her own materials the entire warp and much of the woof which has been woven into this fabric. It is only when some of the less important of the materials seemed to be wanting that the author has felt at liberty to supply them, always adhering as closely as possible to the probabilities and to what he supposed the fact to be.

The author was not present at the numerous interviews between the leading persons and no records exist of their conversations. We know from subsequent events that such conversations were held—they are necessary to the relation. Instead of omitting the language of these interviews and leaving his work imperfect, the author has attempted to supply it. And there were results which must have been preceded by unrecorded causes. Those causes have in a few instances been given as the writer supposes they must have existed. Such is the whole extent to which he has departed from the record. This being understood, it is not believed that the charm which truth gives to every book will be materially diminished, while on the other hand the volume will be rendered more interesting and attractive.

A brief recapitulation will show that the author was under no necessity which called for the invention of facts, and afford another proof that truth is sometimes stranger than fiction.

The Union officer enlisted, served, was desperately wounded, left when the army retired, all as herein stated. In his desolate solitude, when very near to death, he was discovered by the heroine, a young woman who had not completed her nineteenth year, whose husband and brothers were Confederate soldiers; her husband a prisoner. She removed the Union officer to her own dwelling, and with the assistance of the country doctor nursed him back to life. She made journeys to Harper's Ferry for supplies, to Cedar Creek for his clothing. She experienced all the vicissitudes:

aided in his escape and accompanied him to Harper's Ferry and Washington, procured an order for the release of her husband, found him and went to Vermont with the Union officer, all as herein written. Such a plot needs no additions. It is so extraordinary that the author would hesitate to indorse its truth if he had not visited the localities, conversed with the parties, and found it confirmed in so many particulars that to doubt it further would be affectation.

When, through the assistance of Mrs. Van Metre, the Union officer reached Harper's Ferry and was safe within the Union lines, he found that the story of his abandonment and the efficient conduct of his nurse, to which he owed the preservation of his life, was already well known to General Stevenson, then in command at that post. Of his own accord General Stevenson immediately communicated the substance of the story to Secretary Stanton by letter. The answer of the Secretary was an order for the immediate release of Mrs. Van Metre's husband, then supposed to be confined in Fort Delaware. The next day Mrs. Van Metre received by mail the following letter, the original of which has been in the hands of the author of this book. It proves that her conduct was highly appreciated by Secretary Stanton at the time, and is one of the numerous evidences which have been furnished of the truth of the narrative here given.

The letter referred to reads as follows:

"WASHINGTON CITY, D. C.,
"Nov. 4th, 1864.
"MRS. VAN METRE, HARPER'S FERRY.

"*Madam:*—It is with unfeigned pleasure that I comply with the instructions of the Secretary of War and inform you that he has ordered the unconditional discharge of your husband, now at Fort Delaware.

"Mr. Stanton has been sensibly touched by the report received through General Stevenson of your noble and humane conduct toward a wounded Federal officer and soldier, and without a moment's delay has acted upon the suggestion of General Stevenson and ordered the discharge of your husband, as some acknowledgment of the feminine goodness and nobleness manifested in your person.

"If such an example could but extensively find imitations, it would do infinite honor to your sex and greatly relieve war of some of its most barbarous tendencies.

"Very respectfully your obedient servant,
"E. A. HITCHCOCK,
"Maj.-Gen. Vols."

CHAPTER II.

THE VALLEY OF VIRGINIA.

THERE are localities in our favored land which nature has made as beautiful as a poet's dream. In a country which comprises every kind of natural scenery; where mountain, valley, lake, river, and plain are found in every possible combination, no one spot can be selected as the most attractive. Opinions vary. Standing upon the brink of a cañon, looking down along its perpendicular walls to the river bounding over its rocky bed six thousand feet below, then looking upward above the glaciers and eternal snows two miles into the blue ether, one may well say, "This is indeed grand!" The domes of the Yosemite, the geysers of the National Park, the thunders of Niagara, and the sublime scenes where once rolled the Oregon and "heard no sound save his own dashings," fill every beholder with wonder and admiration. To the writer, the great forest which clothes the western slope of the Sierra Nevada is one of the mightiest works of nature. We are now interested in a less imposing but more beautiful picture.

The Shenandoah Valley, otherwise known as the Garden of Virginia, is flanked by two noble mountain ranges extending southward from the Potomac River. Its width varies from twelve to thirty miles. About one-third of its extent from the river another mountain range rises abruptly, converting the one into two valleys. The foot-hills on either side slope gradually away, forming a succession of moderate elevations, between which silvery streams from the mountains drain the region. The valley of the Shenandoah, the Luray, and the other valleys, originally settled by an industrious class of emigrants, have been divided into farms and brought under a high state of cultivation. The primitive forest of oak, chestnut, magnolia, and tulip trees once covered the entire valley and the surrounding mountain slopes. This forest has been largely cleared away, but many noble trees still remain to shade the highways and the grounds about the residences. Broad turnpikes traverse the whole section. There are many passes through the mountains, called "gaps," and in each of these is a highway which bisects the turnpikes. A large river flows through the valley in a very crooked course, furnishing abundant water to the farms, which are also well watered by the streams and creeks from the "gaps" on either side. The main, or Shenandoah valley was the theatre of the principal events which it is our purpose to describe.

In the later days of November, 1860, a geologist and mining engineer just returned from Heidelberg, where he had graduated with honors, was employed to make some explorations in the county of Rockbridge. He had heard such accounts of the region that, being in no especial haste, he determined to approach it from Harper's Ferry on horseback. At that place he hired a horse which proved to be a very fine animal, and sending his trunks and geological tools forward by stage, was ready to begin his journey. But first, from such maps and information as he could collect, he arranged an itinerary which gave him a daily ride of twenty or twenty-five miles, and brought him at evening to some hamlet or village where there was a hotel. He had not yet learned what he soon ascertained, that country hotels were not a necessity, the traveller being welcome at almost any dwelling along the road he was travelling.

He had passed through the quiet town of Charlestown, the capital of Jefferson County, where John Brown attempted his crazy enterprise and met his fate, into the adjoining county of Clarke. Here he was upon the territory originally owned by Lord Fairfax, which was surveyed by Washington before he became eminent as a soldier. The practiced eye of the general appreciated the fertility of the soil, and he became, by purchase from the lord of the manor, the owner of many large tracts of land in this vicinity. Many of his descendants settled upon these lands and some of them occupy them at the present time. From the fine, large, rambling buildings always provided with broad lawns and shaded by noble trees they still dispense that liberal, kindly hospitality which makes a visit to one of these families an oasis in the life of a resident of the city—an event long to be remembered in the journal of the traveller.

Where the turnpike entered the county of Clarke it brought the engineer in view of a scene as beautiful as his eyes had ever beheld. The mountains on either side were covered to their tops with a forest of deciduous trees. Their foliage, now in its ripened maturity, painted the landscape with an exquisite combination of neutral tints and rich colors. Lower down, the foothills gave the country a rolling surface, and among them nestled many a picturesque rural homestead. From the mountains rapid streams dashed over their rocky beds down to the lower lands and then wound their crooked ways between fringes of alder and willow. Around many of the dwellings large trees of primitive growth had been left, to shade the avenues and approaches. Orchards laden with golden fruit were common. The lovely landscape, the pure atmosphere, the blue sky, filled the horseman with new strength and vigor and had a similar effect upon the animal he rode. "This view is worth all the time and cost of my journey," said the horseman to himself, "if I never see the boundary line of Rockbridge County."

He was most impressed, however, by the amazing fertility of the soil. It seemed to be a reddish loam which everywhere produced an abundant harvest. There were few outbuildings, for the climate did not render a warm shelter for the animals in winter a necessity. But in every farm-yard there were many great stacks of hay, grain, corn, and wheat. In the pastures the grass was still abundant for the many horses, cattle, and sheep. Even the swine were permitted to gorge themselves upon the apples which had fallen from the trees. In many fields the laborers were loading great farm wagons with turnips, beets, and potatoes. It was literally a land of abundance.

As he was approaching the town of Berryville, the capital of Clarke County, he noticed a lane leading westward, nearly at right angles to the turnpike, which apparently led to a farm of large size. He was within sight of Berryville, where he intended to pass his first night, and had abundant time. He dismounted, opened the swinging gate, and mounting again, allowed his horse to walk slowly along the lane.

Passing between hedges of the Osage orange, not very well trimmed, where broad fields of wheat and corn had been recently harvested, on either hand, he soon came within view of the residence. It was upon a slight elevation, sloping gently in every direction. The house was only one story high, but it made up in length and breadth what it lacked in height. On the south or front of the house was a velvety lawn, skirted on all sides with grand old oaks, chestnuts, and magnolias. On the north or in the rear were the slaves' quarters and the kitchen, separated from the house. A fine vegetable and fruit garden extended farther in the rear.

The traveller halted under the shade of a grand old chestnut and permitted the beauty of the picture to grow upon his mind. It increased with his inspection. The residence and its surroundings seemed built for that old-time Virginia hospitality of which he had read, but which he had never experienced. He led his horse to a spring which ran across the lane or private road, and while he drank, his rider began to inspect and admire his fine limbs and action. As he patted him gently on the shoulders the animal responded by a gentle whinny, which was immediately answered from a paddock which had been partially hidden from him by the stacks of corn and grain and their protecting thatch of straw. Farther beyond he saw another and a larger field in which there was a herd of cattle.

Himself a farmer's son, the horseman was

skilled in breeds of cattle and horses. Leading his horse, he approached as nearly as possible the first field, in which he saw a picture which at the same time surprised and delighted him. There were ten or a dozen brood-mares and their foals. The action of these colts, so graceful, so quick, so powerful, showed to his practiced eye that while the mares were of the best native breeds, the colts had an infusion of that wonderful Percheron blood which France owed to the first Napoleon, as it did many other of its most profitable advances in the arts, in manufactures, and other departments of human activity as well as in the breeding of horses and cattle.

He had stood for some time witnessing with delight the gambols of the colts and wondering how he could get access to the field beyond, in which he had discovered some fine blooded Ayrshire cows, when looking behind him he found himself very near the rear entrance to the house and grounds. He was immediately surrounded by a flock of woolly-headed, barefooted young darkies, all clamorously proposing to hold his horse, while two or three of the largest actually seized upon his bridle. They were not uncivil; they were decently but not over liberally clothed; their white eye-balls shining in their black faces interested and their antics amused him. He was considering how he could make use of the entire flock without exciting the jealousy of any individual of it, when a stately old colored person came out of the house with an innocent switch in his hand and proceeded to drive away the youngsters.

"Whar you' manners, you sassy imps? Into de quarters, ebery one o' ye. If ye don't I'll thrash ye till the blood runs!" a threat which seemed to amuse the crowd. Then turning to the horseman he said: "I hope you plees scuse de young uns! Dey means well but dey's had no bringin' up. Plees walk into de house. I will care for your animal, sah. De colonel an missus are out in de pike on de saddle-horses. Dey will return berry soon. As soon as I stable you' horse I will show you to your 'partment."

The traveller was so impressed with the unaffected civility of this venerable person of seventy years, whose woolly head was perfectly white, that he did not interrupt him until he was about to take the bridle from his hand. Then he explained that he was a stranger, a traveller through the country who had been attracted by the beauty of the place and wished to have a nearer view of the colts and their dams and the cattle. He was unacquainted with their owner and had no thought of becoming a burden upon his hospitality. If he might be permitted to enter the yard and have a closer view of the colts for a few minutes he would proceed on his journey.

This arrangement was not at all satisfactory to the temporary representative of the house. He insisted that the horse must have his feed—his rider must be weary after his ride of twenty miles from "de Ferry." Lunch was almost ready; "de fambly" would feel hurt if he did not remain until they returned from their ride. He was sincerely grieved when the traveller assured him that his engagements would not permit of a longer delay.

Fastening his bridle to a hitching-post, the old servant led the way to the fields. The closer his inspection the greater was the traveller's pleasure at the sight of the horses and cattle. The field inclosing the Ayrshires comprised the most elevated portion of the farm. Looking northwestward, he saw a smaller farm through which ran a stream of considerable size. At one point where there seemed to be a fall there was a large stone structure surrounded by shade-trees. Beyond it there was a broad, level farm, and beyond this again another farm somewhat broken by hills and apparently pasturing a large number of horses. Upon further inquiry of the venerable servant, he learned that the mill farm, as it was called, was the property of a young bachelor named Van Metre, who resided in a part of the mill finished for a dwelling, to which it was rumored the owner would soon bring its new mistress. The next place was Clifton, and still farther beyond was Claremont, which as he learned from the same informant was a fine farm upon which its proprietor, Colonel Luke, raised some of the finest horses of Virginia.

"And what is the name of this beautiful place where we are standing?" asked the young engineer.

"This is Audley, sah. It is owned by my massa Colonel Lewis, who belongs to de Washington family. He is a grandson of the beautiful Nelly Custis, the grandchile of Missus Washington. We has many tings in de house dat b'longed to her." And pointing to a window he added, "In that room she died. I wish you would stay and meet de colonel and Missus Lewis. You would like de colonel and missus, sir. Everybody likes de colonel and Missus Lewis."

"I have no doubt of that whatever," said the traveller, now rather mortified that he had attempted to seek information of the region from a servant instead of his master. Warmly expressing his thanks for the particulars he had gained, he mounted his horse and rode away in the direction of Berryville.

His bridle-path across the country brought him to a spring, at the head of which he noticed a building of squared timbers about twelve feet in length, dove-tailed at the corners and presenting evidences of great age. The timbers were of chestnut oak, a most durable wood, but into them furrows an inch in depth had been worn by exposure to the winds and weather. Inside, a rude flight of stairs led to the upper room. A trap-door in the floor being raised was directly over the source of the spring. A noble oak shaded the building, and under it a large boulder furnished a convenient seat to the horseman after his horse had drunk his fill at the cool spring.

While he was curious to know for what use such a building could have been constructed, a farmer approached him, who announced himself as the owner of the premises. "It is the current belief in the neighborhood," he said, "that this hut was built by General Washington before his expeditions against the Indians and while he was engaged in surveying these lands for Lord Fairfax, their owner. It is well known that this end of the valley was surveyed by Washington and that he purchased large tracts of these lands from Lord Fairfax, and some of the best farms still remain in the possession of branches of his family. It is said that the upper room was the sleeping-room of his chain-men and that the lower room was occupied by himself. This was one of the farms in the Washington purchase," he continued, "and yonder," pointing to a knoll of moderate height, "is the highest point in the valley between the foot-hills."

The traveller ascended the elevation to which

the farmer pointed and was charmed with the view in every direction. The boundaries of the valley, the gaps in the mountains, and the rivers have already been mentioned. As far as the eye could reach to the southward and limited only by the mountain ranges east and west, he saw farms similar to the one he had left, houses shaded by large trees and almost hidden by the huge stacks of hay and grain that surrounded them. In many of the fields white men and black were contentedly working side by side digging beets, turnips, and potatoes and loading them into huge farm wagons. The farms appeared to be well fenced. In some of the fields horses and in others cows and young cattle were grazing, and all this stock, so far as he could judge, was of the most desirable races and breeds. There was an air of abundance, of plenty, pervading the region which led him to say to himself, "Here is a section of our favored land to which want and hunger, war and its miseries can never come!"

And yet he remembered with a shudder that only twelve months before this whole region had been thrown into the fiercest excitement by the invasion of John Brown and twenty-two other equally insane fanatics. True, the party had been defeated, some shot, others hung, and others had run away, so that none remained to disturb the peace of the valley. He knew, too, that there had recently been an election, that many intemperate threats had been made of the dire results which would follow the election of one or another of the candidates. Surely, he thought, those threats will not be carried into execution. And if war should come it will be restricted to a few armed conflicts in the cities or along the Atlantic coast, and then better counsels will prevail and peace will return. It cannot be that these mountains will ever echo the roar of artillery, that these peaceful farms will become the theatres of bloody battles, or that this lovely landscape will ever be illuminated by the lurid torch of war!

Passing the night in Berryville, our traveller next day pursued his journey. The valley seemed to grow in beauty as it narrowed in extent. Leaving Masanutten like a grand sentinel on his right, he passed down the lovely vale of Luray, halting only long enough to inspect its mighty caverns with their magical effects in the limestone rocks; past the Natural Bridge, Harrisonburg, Staunton, and on to the locality of his investigations in Rockbridge County. The result of his scientific work there was not encouraging to the promoters of the enterprise he was expected to forward. That enterprise received his honest, emphatic condemnation. But he reported to his employers that on his way to Rockbridge County he had traversed, as he believed, the most fertile as it was unquestionably the most exquisitely beautiful valley on the continent of America.

His report to his employers made, he turned his face westward, supposing that he had seen this valley for the last time. But great events were even then maturing in the near future. Had they been disclosed to him, he would within a little more than two years have seen himself returning hither as a general of brigade, now sending the enemy whirling up the valley, again himself sent whirling by the foe down the valley in his turn. He would have seen himself leaving it for the last time as the commander of a division in an army, driving all the horses, cattle, sheep, and swine in their advance, their march illuminated by the conflagration of every outbuilding, of all the stacks of hay and grain, of everything capable of supporting human life. Instead of the pasture of abundance which he saw on his first visit, there would have been a smoking, barren desert, until another season's crop incapable of supporting human life.

The miseries of war force themselves upon a nation in defiance of all resistance. We shall see enough of them in this valley as the incidents of our story are developed without attempting to anticipate them. We will hereafter deal with them as they arise.

CHAPTER III.

A HOME IN VERMONT BEFORE THE WAR.

UNDER the shadow of one of the loftiest peaks of the Green Mountains, well toward the northern boundary of Vermont, is situated the township which I shall call Westfield. There are many such towns on the flanks of the Green Mountains. They are formed by a combination of hill and valley, too much of the first and too little of the second. The rugged shoulders of the mountains extend at right angles to the principal range, and the rivers between them, which spread below into broad, rich intervals, are here only trout-brooks dashing along their rocky beds. There are here and there small areas capable of cultivation, but the greater part of the lands when cleared are fit only for pasturage.

These are literally mountain towns. The primitive forest which originally covered the country, in the valleys where there was some depth of soil, comprised the soft and the sugar maple, the beech, and two or three birches of average size. These upon the hillsides were gradually replaced by the hemlock and spruce, which became less in diameter with the ascent until on the mountain-tops they were dwarfed into impenetrable thickets. The first to attack these forests were the lumbermen, who felled and carried away the trees large enough for sawing, and then usually permitted the lands to revert to the State upon sales for unpaid taxes. Later these lands became of some value on account of the scarcity and increased price of charcoal, and still later they were farther increased by the demand for wood pulp. In 1860 they were not worth more than three or four dollars per acre.

In one of the poorest of these mountain towns lived Farmer Bedell, a lineal descendant of an ancestor who came over in the *Mayflower*, and who, if he had not inherited the persistence, the industry, and the religion of his ancestor, could never have raised a family and maintained a decent respectability upon the barren soil which he had cleared from the forest and called his farm. I shall not attempt to explain why Bedell and others like him, when the rich prairies of the West and even of the Genesee Country were open to the emigrant, located here, where the soil was so unproductive and the climate so cold that their stock must be sheltered and fed for one-half the year; fortunate if they could glean their living for the other half from the stony hillsides. Perhaps the correct explanation was given by one of them to a traveller who asked him what they raised in such a barren country. "We raise men," was his reply, and it was a true answer. There are hundreds of men who in enterprise, energy, and learning have honored the American name, distancing their competitors in all the departments of human industry and usefulness, who were born and reared in just such mountain towns.

Bedell married, and sons and daughters were born to him. Our story concerns only Henry, a son who was born in 1834. He began to be useful to his father at the age of seven years, and his usefulness increased until he left the homestead. During the three winter months he went to the district school. The nine remaining months of the year he labored for his father, who was the lawful owner of his time and services until he had completed his twenty-first year. At the age of eighteen, like many other Vermont boys, he purchased the remainder of his minority from his father, agreeing to give him three hundred dollars for it. He was six feet tall, strong and vigorous, for he had never abused his health. Except to watch by a sick friend he had never been awake at midnight in his life. He could now cut a broader swath in the hay-field, he could cradle more acres of wheat, he could cut more cord-wood in a day, than any other man in his town. His labor was in demand, for he was as faithful as he was strong. For the greater part of the year he earned and his employers paid him as much as a dollar a day for his work from sunrise to sunset. He never complained, never struck or even agitated for higher wages, but went straight on. At the age of twenty-one he had paid his father for his time and was the owner of one hundred acres of as good land as there was in the township of Westfield.

Then the forest began to fall before the strokes of his powerful axe, the trees were cut into even lengths, made into log-heaps and burned. The ashes were collected and sold to the maker of potash. In the fall he sowed a small field of winter wheat, and the next spring he planted his first crop of corn, potatoes, turnips, etc. He could afford to hire a carpenter, and in his leisure hours between planting and hoeing he built a good, warm, substantial log-house. To this house one morning in June he brought his wife and her dowry. That of such a Vermont bride was neither costly nor comprehensive. It usually comprised a chest of drawers, a bedstead, a few chairs, a wooden clock, some cheap crockery, and other necessaries given by her father. The family jewels, consisting of a string of gold beads, and a Bible, were the gifts of the mother. Linen sheets and pillow-cases spun and woven with her own hands, blankets made with the assistance of her mother, her own wardrobe for a year purchased with her wages as the teacher of a district school, together with the contributions of her husband, made a very fair outfit for the young couple. She was a good, wholesome Vermont girl, wholesome in her heart and soul as well as in her person, fitted by training and an education almost self-won to be the wife of a true man and the mother of his children.

As we shall see much of Bedell in the course of our story, we shall leave his character as it is developed to the judgment of the reader. But a word or two must be written about his personal appearance. In height and strength he was gigantic. He now measured six feet two inches in his stockings, and he was in every limb and muscle well proportioned. His face always wore a kind and genial expression, intensified possibly by his gentle blue eyes and light brown hair. His hands and feet were well formed, his movements so easy that he seemed to do everything without exertion.

Of necessity the young couple prospered. They were both attentive and helpful to all their neighbors, especially to those who were in distress or want. We will not follow the details of their lives. They were not unusual or extraordinary. There have been hundreds of such lives in New England, where they are too common to attract notice.

In that November when the mining engineer is travelling through the valley of Virginia, the

Bedells of our story have been married six or seven years. Three children have been born to them, of whom both father and mother are just a little proud. The youngest of these is only five months old. They have adopted an orphan, son of a deceased Bedell, who has reached the age of ten years and is as dear to them as if he was their own son. He is a bright lad, competent to look after the farm while his adopted father is away. In these seven years the world has gone well with them. He has brought as much of his farm under cultivation as he thinks profitable, and has added another to it which produces an unusually large crop of hay. Both farms now constitute one, which is well stocked with cattle, sheep, and horses. He has barn room for his entire crop of hay and grain and a warm shelter in the long, cold winter for every animal he owns. The log-house has disappeared. In its place stands a neat farm-house, one and a half stories high, with its "square room," bedrooms, and kitchen well furnished and provided with all approved modern conveniences. He has no dairy, for his milk is sent to the creamery, that greatest boon to the New England wife. There is a bookcase well stocked —he takes an agricultural as well as the county paper. While he devotes himself to his farm, his wife, besides being a most excellent housekeeper, is a faithful mother to her children and is their daily teacher. Henry Bedell is not only a selectman, but he is the leading citizen and his farm is one of the best in the township. He would have represented his town in the State legislature this year if his neighbors could have had their choice. But he is a man of firmness who has a singular habit of considering the claims of other men before his own. There was a neighbor who was entitled to the place, he said, and he could afford to wait. The neighbor is the representative, but he is also a friend who would go through fire to serve Bedell. And so it happens that husband and household are a credit to the State and their town. The husband is an industrious, charitable, benevolent citizen. His wife is a pattern for other wives, affectionate and useful. There are none better in the Republic than these farmers of the mountain towns of Vermont, of whom it is not claimed that the Bedells are more than average examples.

CHAPTER IV.

THE TRUMPET-CALL OF WAR IN THE GREEN MOUNTAINS.

The red tongue of war licked the walls of Sumter and his brazen throat belched out a roar which rolled up every New England valley, out over every Western prairie. There followed it the call for men. Henry E. Bedell scarcely noted the sound of the guns, but the call for men touched every nerve in his giant frame. It was in the spring-time, when he was ploughing and sowing and planting. While he reflected upon his duty, the call was filled by prompter men and the demand had passed him by. Then there came disaster and defeat—another call, sharper, more peremptory, not to be disregarded by one who loved his country. Once more the Vermont farmer looked upon his wife and home, and while he hesitated other and apparently more patriotic men had responded, and again he felt that he had failed of his duty. "But in the sultry summer-time, as war's red records show," of 1862, came that memorable appeal to which no loyal ear was deaf, no loyal heart failed to respond. It was the call for "three hundred thousand more." "From Mississippi's winding stream to far New England's shore," no ear was quicker to hear, no heart more prompt to answer than the ear and heart of the Westfield farmer. It came to him in his county paper early one morning. Instantly he decided that this call was for him and he would answer it, not by any cheap substitute, but in person. Then his mind was at rest. He went out into the morning air. Never did his eye rest more longingly upon his farm, his animals, his home. He entered his dwelling. His children clamorously demanded their daily privilege of climbing upon his shoulders. They performed the feat and proclaimed their achievement with shouts of joy and kisses of love. His wife saw upon his face a look which she had never witnessed before. She followed him into another apartment. Without a word he drew her to him with one arm, holding in his other hand the open paper. With a woman's intuition she understood it all. "I cannot hold you back, Henry! I would not if I could," she said. "The country needs you and you must go. But, O God, preserve my husband!" she cried, struggling to keep down the wave of fear which threatened to overwhelm her when she most wished for strength.

"Heaven bless you, my brave wife," he said, controlling his own emotion with a mighty effort. "I knew you would not fail me in this crisis.

And now, dear, let us sit down and talk it all over calmly. I have been expecting this call, and the devil has been very busy in devising ways for me to avoid it. He suggests that I can hire a substitute who has no wife and children to suffer if he loses his life. It is my first duty, he urges, to stay at home and take care of my family. I need not repeat his arguments or my replies. The country is in danger. It wants strong, earnest, healthy men, and not cheap substitutes who will desert or run away at the first opportunity. I am strong and healthy, and at least I ought to be big enough to be of some use to my country," he continued, casting a glance over his gigantic frame and forcing himself to smile. "These misguided men at the South must be defeated if they persist in their efforts to break up the Government, and I must help to do it. I should despise myself, earn the contempt of all honest men, and dishonor my native State if I did not obey this call!"

"You are right, Henry," she replied. "If I were a man I should feel as you do, and I almost wish I were one, so that I might go with you and fight by your side. But my place is here, to care for our children and to pray for you. God will watch over us and reunite us. I feel it, and I will not make the parting harder by a single tear."

Afraid to trust herself to say more, the brave

wife hurried from the room and threw herself heart and soul into the preparations for her husband's departure. Whatever may have been her secret anguish, not a trace of it appeared upon her calm, serene brow when her dear ones were by. An atmosphere of somewhat forced cheerfulness pervaded the household, even the little ones taking an active part in the work of preparation. Imitating their mother's example, they endeavored to appear happy and unconcerned as they went about the work of cleaning, brushing, and polishing which fell to their share. But, young as they were, they felt the sad undercurrent beneath the assumed cheerfulness about them, and often the merry laugh would cease and a silent tear fall at the thought that "father was going to the war."

On the 4th day of August, 1862, Bedell with dry eyes and a strong heart took leave of his family and his Westfield home, and enlisted in Company D, Eleventh Vermont Volunteers. He was such a magnificent specimen of manhood that on the day of his enlistment his captain insisted upon promoting him, and he was borne on the roster as Corporal Bedell. On the first day of September his regiment was mustered into the service of the United States. James M. Warner, a lieutenant in the regular army and an educated soldier, was its colonel. The regiment was ordered first to Washington, where it became a regiment of heavy artillery, and being separated into batteries of one hundred and fifty men was distributed into the forts which protected the capital. There it served for eighteen long months and until April, 1864.

This may have been a useful service, but it was not liked by officers or men. They seemed to be wasting time in idleness which should have been in some way made profitable to the cause.

But Corporal Bedell was a true soldier, content to obey his superior officers and to perform the duty which they assigned to him. He had one privilege of which he availed himself almost daily. Everything known to the corporal was promptly communicated to his wife and neighbors in their Vermont homes.

Then on the 11th of August, all unconscious that he had done anything but his daily duty, he was informed that he had been again promoted and that he was now Sergeant Bedell. His surprise was greater when, on the 28th of December, 1863, while the regiment was still in the defences of Washington, he was deemed worthy of a commission. On the 12th of January, 1864, he received his commission as lieutenant. About the same time Aldace Walker, who had joined the regiment as a lieutenant, was made its lieutenant-colonel. This story cannot turn aside to do justice to Colonel Walker. I may, however, take this occasion to say that the subsequent very lively and magnificent fighting of the regiment was under Colonel Walker's command, that he was deservedly breveted as colonel for his personal bravery, and that he is now the chairman of the Interstate Railway Association of the United States.

The record of the regiment covers gallant service at Spottsylvania, May 15th to 18th; Cold Harbor, June 1st to 12th; Petersburg, June 18th; Weldon Railroad, June 23d; Fort Stevens, in front of Washington, July 12th, 1864. Then it went into the Shenandoah Valley and fought in all the battles there under Sheridan. Its history has been written by Colonel Walker, and we shall follow it so far as it is connected with the heroine of our story and Lieutenant Bedell.

CHAPTER V.

THE CALL TO ARMS IN THE VALLEY.

No man of Northern birth or sympathies should undertake to describe from a Southern standpoint the war in the valley of Virginia. It may be permitted to the writer to say that a strong sentiment in favor of the Union was supposed to exist in the State and was loyally entertained by a large majority of the people of the valley, including all citizens of the better class. But the guns of Sumter struck the note of separation. When General Lee resigned from the army of the United States and consented to take command of the Confederate army of Virginia, the Union sentiment immediately and completely disappeared. Nowhere did the Confederate call for recruits meet with a more general and cordial response than in the Shenandoah Valley. One of the earliest to volunteer had been J. L. E. Van Metre, the owner of the estate of which we have already attempted a slight description.

He had enlisted in the Confederate army in the summer of 1861, when there was supposed to be little danger that the wave of war would reach the valley. His horses, cattle, and other animals had been purchased by the Confederate Government and paid for in money and bonds. There was supposed to be little left worth the trouble of capture. The homestead was therefore left in charge of Peter Dennis, a faithful colored slave, with Mrs. Betty Van Metre and her young niece as its tenants.

But the valley of Virginia proved to be one of the great highways of civil war. From its productive capacity the Confederacy was to derive a large proportion of its provisions. Its people could temporarily leave the service in the spring, raise and harvest a crop, and return to active service in the autumn. Therefore the tidal wave of war annually and sometimes quarterly rolled up and down the valley, every time engulfing the Van Metre homestead, until nearly every useful animal, every wheeled vehicle, all the hay, straw, in short, almost everything portable had been swept away. Even the able-bodied slaves had been sent as laborers to the Confederate front. The mill and outbuildings had so far escaped destruction or much injury. As "single misfortunes do not come alone," in the summer of 1864 Van Metre was captured and became a prisoner to the Union forces.

We will not undertake to follow the Northern army, which under the command of Sheridan "went into" the valley early in August, 1864.

On the 10th of that month his whole command moved out of Harper's Ferry and went into camp at Clifton, a large plantation near Berryville. Here and hereabout the Vermont brigade remained for several days. It came to the knowledge of some of the officers of that brigade that in the stone mill and dwelling already mentioned, Mrs. Van Metre, the wife of the owner, with her young niece and an old colored servant, was living alone and unprotected. Over this homestead they stationed and maintained a guard which secured it against further intrusion. To show her gratitude for such protection, Mrs. Van Metre suggested that while she had no provisions of her own, she might prepare their army rations in a manner which would remind them of the cooking of their wives and daughters at home. The officers accordingly sent her their beef, bacon, and hard-tack, and adding a few vegetables from her own garden she prepared for them several dinners. These dinners so spread her reputation as a cook that until the brigade moved away her table was filled daily with as many guests as she could accommodate. The officers were all gentlemen, who treated her with the respect they would have demanded for their mothers or their wives, and the dinners became memorable. When they went to the field, many of them to their deaths, there was not one who did not carry with him a profound respect for Mistress

Betty Van Metre. How far she remembered them we shall learn hereafter.

The time of his or her introduction into a story is usually the occasion for the description of the principal character. In the course of this narrative the reader will form a very intimate acquaintance with Mrs. Betty Van Metre. I prefer to leave him to form his own opinion of her without any influence of mine. I shall give a very brief sketch of her origin and her life up to her nineteenth year, when she becomes more actively connected with this history. Beyond that I shall leave her to be known and judged by her own conduct—her own construction of the duty of a true woman.

CHAPTER VI.

HOW A BRAVE MAN MET THE HEAVY STROKE OF MERCILESS WAR.

OUR story is now touched by the bloody hand of active War. The Vermont brigade, to which Bedell's regiment was attached, belonged to the division then commanded by that brave and popular officer General Getty. The division was in camp on the farm called Claremont, about three miles north from Berryville and about two miles west of the turnpike from Harper's Ferry through Charlestown and thence up the valley. Winchester, the largest city in the lower valley, lies ten and a half miles due west from Berryville on another turnpike. About half-way from Berryville to Winchester, the road by a ford crosses the Opequan (pronounced Opeccan) Creek, which runs northerly into the Potomac at Williamsport. The banks of this creek are high and bold, and in high water the ford is frequently impassable.

On the morning of September 13th, 1864, the division of General Getty moved out toward the Opequan to ascertain the position of the army of

General Early, then known to be on the west bank of that river. The Vermont brigade had the advance, the third and fourth regiments being deployed as skirmishers. There were no fences, and the force moved directly across the country about five miles to the creek. Sheridan and Wright accompanied the column.

The skirmishers reached and forded the creek, meeting the Confederate pickets a short distance up and beyond the west bank. Captain Cowan's battery went into position on the east side of the creek and opened fire, hoping thus to discover the enemy's camps in that vicinity and their numerical strength. This battery was in plain view from the opposite side. There was an occasional shot from the rifles of the skirmishers in advance of Cowan's battery on the west bank of the creek, and the rest of the division was massed in a wood a quarter of a mile behind the battery. This wood was free from underbrush; it afforded an excellent shade; the men were scattered in groups among the stacked rifles, conversing or otherwise amusing themselves.

It is now known from Major More, the officer upon the staff of General Early who carried the order, that the fire from Cowan's battery having become annoying, General Early ordered up a heavier battery on the west side of the creek, to silence Cowan's guns or compel him to retire. The first shells from the Confederate guns were fired at too high an elevation, passed over the guns at which they were aimed, and exploded among the tree-tops, doing no further injury. But this error was soon corrected, and the shells began to plough through and explode among the ranks of the division concealed in the timber. Several were wounded; the lines were formed for removal to some safer position. But as the enemy's missiles began to fall short of the Unionists, they became satisfied that their exact position was unknown to the enemy, and in a few minutes the firing ceased and danger was over.

Bedell always set a good example before his men when under fire. As an officer he deemed it his duty to take good care of his men and not to attempt concealment of his own person. His great height, his muscular activity, and splendid physique made him an attractive target, of which the enemy did not fail to avail themselves. He was bravely holding his men in line, when the guns in the Confederate battery were concentrated upon him; one shell exploded, tearing his right hand, leaving three fingers each hanging by its tendons, and he fell. A second shell had crashed through his left thigh, leaving a portion of the muscle on either side, and a horrible mass of crushed bones, mangled flesh, and gushing arteries in its pathway.

As he fell and saw the bright red blood spurting from the severed arteries, he made a brave attempt to compress his thigh with his uninjured and his mangled hand, for he knew that a brief delay involved his death. It was ineffectual, for there was but little strength in that fragment of a hand. "Cord it, boys!" he exclaimed as he lay upon the ground. "Don't let me bleed to death! Cord it! with a handkerchief or anything, quick! A ramrod and a handkerchief will do it!"

Willing hands tied the handkerchief, but they were nervous and the rude substitute gave way under the too sudden twist, and again the scarlet torrent burst out, impelled by the powerful pulsations of his vigorous heart. "Try it once more, boys!" he exclaimed. "Try a bayonet the next time—it's my only chance!" A young officer tore his sash from his own shoulders, passed it twice around the limb, tied it, another inserted a bayonet, and with a single powerful twist the success of the improvised torniquet was complete—the bleeding was arrested and for the moment his life was saved.

He was more than five miles from the camp to which the division was about to return. They bore him on a stretcher to a temporary field hospital, where the surgeons began to debate whether there was anything to be gained by an amputation. It was a most difficult operation at the best. Weakened by his other wounds, they feared he might die under the surgeon's knife.

The brave man promptly settled the question.

"Is it not certain that this wound will be fatal if the leg is not amputated?" he asked. They agreed it was. "Then lose not a moment's time," he said. "There is a chance of recovery if the leg is amputated—there is none if it is not. In such a case I take the chance!"

They laid him upon the table and the skilled hands of the surgeons of the Vermont brigade performed the amputation. Everything was done for him that could be suggested by science and skill, and the sufferer was made as comfortable as the rude conditions of war permitted. "Still," said the account of Colonel Walker, "there was very little hope. Though his native vigor was in his favor, his very size and the muscular strength upon which he had prided himself were against him, for it was computed that *over sixty-four square inches* of flesh were severed and laid bare by the surgeon's knife. And it was also found that his right hand had been terribly injured, the bones of three fingers and of the middle hand having been crushed and comminuted. The operation already performed had been so severe that it was thought best not to attempt the treatment of the hand until it was seen whether or not he would rally from the shock of the wounds and the amputation."

About dusk the army returned to their camp at Claremont. That journey was a terrible ordeal to the wounded man. It would have been severe enough if his ambulance had moved over an ordinary turnpike road for that distance immediately after he had undergone such a fearful trial. But there were no fences left and few cross-roads. The army moved as the crow flies, straight across the country, over stone walls half torn down, across ditches half filled with broken timbers. Thus jolted and shaken, an ordinary life would have inevitably been destroyed. But Bedell's was not an ordinary life. He determined to live if he could. Sustained by stimulants and his indomitable courage, at last in the darkness he reached the camp of the division alive.

A short distance eastward from the camp, on another farm, was a house which had been deserted by the owner and his family. The basement was occupied by an old man and his wife, both apparently destitute of human hearts and sympathies. Tempted by the promise of rewards, they consented that Bedell should be placed in one of the unoccupied rooms of the second story of the house, and then, having made him as comfortable as they could, his companions left him for the night, scarcely expecting that the morning sun would see him alive.

The next morning the surgeon of his regiment found him not only alive, but stronger than he was the evening before. After an examination and the statement that he was delighted to see him feeling better, he was about to leave, when Bedell said to him:

"Surgeon, you doctors think I have got my fatal wound—that I cannot live. You propose to make my short journey to the grave as easy as possible. I know perfectly well that the chances are against me. But I have got a wife and children up in Vermont who want me. I want to live on my own account—much more on theirs. I am going to make the hardest fight for life of which I am capable. I want you to help me. I want you to bring the surgeons of the Fourth and Fifth Vermont right here as soon as you can. I want to talk the matter over and see what can be done to save me."

"I will do it. God knows if you die it shall not be for want of anything that I can do for you," said the surgeon.

By nine o'clock the surgeon of his own regiment and three others were in consultation over him. He insisted that they should discuss the case in his presence. The surgeon of his own regiment, the youngest of the four, alone expressed any hope. The three others said that such an amputation, almost at the very hip, was fatal in the majority of cases without other complications. In this case it was complicated with the wounded hand and the want of hospital accommodations; and there were other reasons why they considered his case hopeless.

The younger man said but little. Bedell waited until none of the surgeons had anything to add. Then, as coolly as if he were speaking of another, he said:

"Gentlemen, my life is not my own property. For another year it belongs to the United States. After that my wife and children own it. I shall save it if I can. I shall not throw away one chance to save it. I decide to place myself in the hands of the surgeon of my own regiment. I know he will do all he can for me. I want one of you to write for me a letter to my wife. Then I will put myself under his direction."

"I will write for you—I will do anything that man can do for you," said the elder of the surgeons, "for you deserve to live." He drew a table to the side of the wounded man and wrote to his wife from his dictation what might prove to be his last letter. It told her the simple truth. He had been desperately wounded—his right leg had been amputated—he was about to undergo another operation, which might terminate his life. Still he had some hope. He gave her plain directions about closing his estate and the education of the children. Its closing words were so touching that he alone of those present was able to control his emotions. There ran through it a single ray of hope, so faint at times that it was scarcely visible. It was just possible that he might survive the operation about to be performed. It was a model letter of a fearless soldier and a loving husband writing to his wife for the last time. With his left hand, assisted by the surgeon, he wrote what bore some resemblance to his name, saw the letter sealed and directed. The older surgeon promised to mail it, and then, turning to the surgeon of the Eleventh Vermont, Bedell said, "Doctor, I am ready."

The young surgeon did not flinch. They brought in a table and laid the wounded man upon it. Bedell watched the preparations with the coolness of a disinterested spectator. But when they offered him the anæsthetic, he declined to take it. He preferred to retain his consciousness.

"The amputation and dressing of your wounded hand and the dressing of your amputated thigh will be tedious and exhausting," said the surgeon. "We must husband every ounce of your strength. You will require it all, and whether it will prove sufficient God only knows."

To this argument Bedell promptly yielded. The blessed boon, which has spared humanity such a vast amount of pain, was administered and the wounded man became unconscious.

The writer is not a surgeon, and if he were he does not know that the description of the long and careful process of amputating the fingers, repairing the stump of the hand, and dressing the thigh would be interesting to his readers. The hand proved to have been reduced to a shapeless mass of fractured bone, crushed muscle, veins and arteries, and severed nerves. The surgeon was skilful and worked with rapidity. But it was a full hour after the patient was laid upon the table before the operation was completed.

A narrow bed filled with straw and laid upon the floor, in a room from which everything even to the window-shades had been removed, was the only couch they could procure for the wounded man. His covering was an army blanket. To this bed they returned him in the bloody clothing worn when he fell. Had Bedell been in his mountain home, or in a hospital where he could have had proper care and a comfortable bed, his subsequent experience showed that he would have had an uninterrupted progress toward recovery. Even here the surgeon hoped that he might secure the constant attendance of a nurse, the dressing of his wounds as often as was necessary, and the regular administration of stimulants and of strengthening food. After a few days' rest he could be removed to Harper's Ferry, where he could be supplied with every necessity. He then explained to Bedell the treatment he intended should be pursued, provided him with refreshing food, placed him in charge of a soldier nurse, and left him for the night.

CHAPTER VII.

DESERTED.

When at sunrise the next morning the surgeon made an early call, he was delighted to find his patient's condition greatly improved. He had had a fair night's rest. His appetite was good and he was free from pain. He complimented Bedell upon his vigorous constitution, which with proper assistance he believed would carry him through to perfect recovery. He informed him that he had made a requisition upon the agency of the Sanitary Commission at Harper's Ferry for a cot bedstead and other conveniences, which would be received in the course of three or four days. Until then the same course of treatment already adopted was to be pursued.

Both the surgeon and Bedell were conscious that his struggle for life had only just begun. In cases of severe wounds like his, nature mercifully provides a torpidity of the nerves which renders them for a short time almost insensible to pain. But when the parts become inflamed there is an increased sensitiveness and the pain is sometimes almost intolerable. This inflammation in Bedell's case was certain to occur, though it was hoped to keep it under control by careful treatment and constant attention.

For two or three days the case progressed as well as the surgeon expected. There was considerable inflammation, but the patient remained perfectly quiet, and by constant bathing and other applications the pain was kept under control. He was growing stronger and progressing steadily toward recovery.

But there were several incidents of Bedell's situation which were very unsatisfactory. The November storms were commencing; the room he occupied was open in many places to the weather and there was no way of heating it. The old couple named Asbury, who were probably trespassers in the basement, but who claimed to have been left in possession by the owner, proved to be human only in form and apparently destitute of all human sympathy. They promised when paid in advance to attend upon Bedell's wants and to prepare his food, but as soon as the surgeon's nurse withdrew they appropriated his supplies and then gave him no farther attention. The house was far enough away from the camp at Claremont to make it an attraction to the guerillas then roving over the country, and no ordinary guard was an adequate security against them.

Finding that the Asburys were more likely to

betray Bedell to some of their friends who were marauding the country than they were to do anything to assist him, the surgeon determined to rely upon a guard from the camp to nurse and protect his patient. But it was not many days before even this precarious protection had to be withdrawn. An advance movement of the Union army was about to take place, and by way of preparation for it, peremptory orders were issued that all the sick and wounded should be at once removed to the hospital at Harper's Ferry, more than twenty miles away.

The heart of the young surgeon sank at the prospect for poor Bedell. He did not believe that he could endure the pain of transportation even for a mile, and to leave him was to abandon him to certain death. Mosby, a daring partisan leader, was always close upon the rear of a retreating Federal army, ready to dash upon it at the first opening. He had captured officers in towns when they were surrounded by their own men. Under the claim that Custer had executed some of his men on the ground that they were not regularly enlisted in the Confederate army, Mosby by way of retaliation had just hung five Union soldiers on the same tree. A Federal officer captured by Mosby, well or wounded, would probably have short shrift. Nor were Mosby's men the worst of the marauders. The caves in the mountains were literally swarming with the most abandoned species of wretches ever created in the human form. They comprised all the criminals of the region, with recruits of men who had fled from the draft, bounty-jumpers, deserters, and vagabonds of all kinds. Some were counterfeiters, some illicit distillers—all thieves and robbers and, upon any prospect of gain, murderers. They were impartial—they robbed both sides; no one who had anything to lose was safe from their bloody knives. There were other wretches in the towns who gave them notice of any possible victim and with whom they divided their spoils. They promptly appeared on every battle-field and murdered the wounded; it was unsafe to travel any road after nightfall, for to encounter them was death. Compared with the operations of these outlaws, bushwhacking was Christian warfare.

It would be more merciful to shoot the wounded officer upon his pallet of straw than to leave him to the mercy of these miscreants. Every effort for his safe removal must be exhausted before that alternative could be considered.

These sudden and unexpected movements are among the most cruel incidents of war. They always cost many lives. The wounded are taken from comfortable beds when their cases are favorably progressing, crowded into army wagons and ambulances and hurried away over the rough and broken roads, too many of them to their deaths. On this occasion the procession that moved northward was not large, for as yet there had been no great battle since this army entered the valley.

An earnest and careful attempt was made to remove Bedell. The ambulance was cushioned, he was carried very gently and laid on a bed on the floor of the vehicle. But now all his wounds had become inflamed and every injured nerve and severed muscle was in angry rebellion. The ambulance moved very slowly, but the shaking and jolting as the wheels fell into well-worn ruts or over obstructions were unavoidable. For a time he bore the pain without a murmur. He uttered no complaint—not a groan escaped him. But the tax was more than he could bear. There was a shiver—his face turned an ashen color, and he fainted. So far as his own suffering was concerned he was dead.

The ambulance was moved out of the procession into a field; the officers of his regiment and his friends gathered about him. What was to be done? To persist in the attempt to remove him would be fatal. He would die before he had made one mile of the twenty. To leave him would expose him to a death almost equally certain. The horizon of his fate seemed closing in on every side.

During the conference Bedell recovered his consciousness. Again his clear judgment considered the situation and decided what should be done. He could not be removed, for he had not the strength to survive the journey. One man like himself must not obstruct the movement of an army. There was only one thing to be done. They must return him to his pallet of straw, arrange whatever they could for his protection, and leave him to take his chance of life, however small it might seem to be.

They replaced him upon his straw mattrass, nearer to death than he had been at any time before. But he had brother-officers who would not abandon him. His desertion might be excused as a cruel necessity, they said, but it would be none the less the act of cowards. As soon as our army retired the scavengers of the camp and field would spread over the country. They took no prisoners, left no living witnesses of their atrocities. If Bedell was left alone they would murder him. But they would not attack two or three determined men.

Bedell calmly told them that after that day's experience he had little hope of recovery; that obviously there was only one possible course, they must leave him; a soldier might remain with him if they thought best; they could give him some supplies, and that was all they could do. When they got to Harper's Ferry, if he lived, they could consult about his further removal.

Bedell so calmly took upon himself as his obvious duty as a soldier all the risks of the situation that his brother-officers yielded, although one of them said that in so doing he felt as if he deserved to be kicked out of camp by a mule. They selected as his nurse a man not in uniform, arranged a box of crackers so that it raised the head of his bed, and placed within his reach vessels of water and cooked food enough to sustain life for several days. The surgeon determined to make one more effort to secure the services of the Asburys. He knew they were faithless, but he hoped to secure their services by partial payment and the promise of future rewards. They promised; they accepted his money; they agreed to visit Bedell hourly—to prepare his food and to do everything he required.

Having made these arrangements, the best that the circumstances admitted, the surgeon and his brother-officers bade the wounded man farewell and took their unwilling leave. A short distance from the house they passed the small dwelling of a colored man who stood at his open door. "What is your name, uncle?" asked the surgeon.

"My name is Dick Runner, suh," he civilly answered.

"What is your work, and is this your house?" pursued the inquirer.

"I work for Missus Van Metre in the mill. Me and Ginny, my wife, have lived here all our lives, suh."

"Uncle," said the surgeon, holding up two bright, new greenbacks, "these are for you. In that room" (pointing to one he had just left) "is a wounded Union officer. I want you to go and see him every morning and see that he wants for nothing. Will you do so?"

"I will see de Union officer ebery day, suh, but I cannot take pay for it. I know what for he come here. He is one of Lincoln's men. Me an' Ginny will do all we can for him, but not for money—no, not for money."

"Then take the money and buy medicines for him," said the surgeon. "We have to leave him to go with the army. The Asburys have promised to care for him, but we do not like to trust them. We think if you promised you would keep your word."

"Dem Asburys is no good, suh. Dey're squatters. Dey've got no business in dat house. You can't trust 'em. But me an' Ginny will do what we can for de wounded officer. But we don' want no pay. What for you didn't see Missus Van Metre? She's a woman an' a lady, is Missus Van Metre. She will help anybody dat's in trouble."

"We cannot wait now to see anybody. Our regiment is already miles away, uncle!" said the surgeon, much impressed by the simple honesty of the colored man. "We wish you would take some money, and look after our brother-officer.

You would relieve our minds if you would, for it cuts us to the heart to leave him, and we fear he is near his end."

But Uncle Dick was obstinate. He would do all he could for the wounded man, but he would not take money. As the surgeon shook his honest hand and with the other grasped that of Ginny, he left in hers a roll of paper covering a small sum in greenbacks, and before she could recover from her surprise enough to protest, he had hurried away.

With the retirement of the army began a time of physical and mental anxiety and distress for Bedell which no pen can adequately describe. The army retired to Harper's Ferry. When it again advanced, Martinsburg, farther west, became its base of supplies, and the region around Berryville, instead of being traversed every few days by army trains, was not again visited for many weeks by Union troops. This part of Clarke County became the hunting-ground for guerillas, camp-followers, tramps, and deserters. Bushwhacking, robbing, and murder were too common to attract attention. The tramps expected no quarter and gave none. Two or three times Custer's cavalry swept over the county, and left the murderers they captured hanging from the trees along the turnpike. Every Union soldier who fell into the hands of the roving murderers was hung or shot as soon as he had been robbed. For the first few days the house where Bedell lay escaped their visitations. It was some distance away from the turnpike and was supposed to have been deserted. Several of these parties were turned away by the apparent stupidity of Uncle Dick Runner, who always contrived to intercept and show them that there was no spoil here, but that there were fresh fields and pastures new in some other direction.

When the officers of Bedell's regiment parted from him they had almost no hope that he would survive. The strain of his attempted removal had been very injurious. They were not much surprised, therefore, when the nurse left with him, two or three days afterward, came into the camp at Harper's Ferry and announced that Bedell had died and he had seen him buried that morning!

This is what had in fact taken place: The nurse had been very brave before the army left. Immediately after its departure he began to show his cowardice. He had heard that an attack was to be made that night—one man could make no defence against guerillas! In short, his cowardly fear so wrought upon Bedell in his nervous condition that he begged the fellow to clear out and leave him. His absence he might survive—his presence he could not endure. The coward left immediately, and to excuse his own conduct circulated the report that Bedell was dead.

The wounded man's next ill-fortune was with

the Asburys, who lived in the basement and claimed to be the landlords of the deserted house. He knew that they had been paid for taking care of him and had promised his friends to attend to his wants. When, therefore, the male Asbury came for his supplies, promising to cook him a meal, he did not object to their being taken away, leaving only the box of crackers, his substitute for a pillow, which did not attract Mr. Asbury's notice. The patient's provisions being thus secured, the inhuman wretch left him to his fate, and Bedell never saw either of the Asburys again.

All through the darkness of that last long and gloomy night the sufferer tossed upon his bed of straw. Hope had not wholly deserted him. "Surely," he thought, "they will at least bring me my breakfast." But the hours passed; they did not come, and then the helpless invalid knew that he was deserted.

Two days and two very long nights had passed since he said farewell to his friends—it was now late in the evening of the third day. I shall not shock the sensibility of my readers by a description of Bedell's sufferings during this time. It will suffice to simply outline his situation. He was helpless from desperate wounds; he was not only in the country of a political enemy, but in a region controlled by the enemies of the human race. He was lying on a straw bed, on the floor of an unfurnished room, through the walls of which the rains beat and the winds whistled. He could not move without a deathly spasm of pain. He had been robbed of his supplies. By an effort which almost exhausted his remaining strength, his single hand had got access to the box of crackers under his head, or he would have already starved. The guerillas would soon be upon him, for those who would steal his food would betray him to the enemy. If they did not, his wounds were every hour becoming more inflamed and more painful, and their pain could not be much longer endured.

Then his thoughts went to his mountain home —to the wife and children who were this night remembering him in their prayers, but, alas! whom he should never see again. What would he not give for the strength to write them one last word, the power to give them one last counsel!

So much as that he would try to do. In the pocket of his vest there was a lead-pencil. With this, on the cover of his cracker-box, he would write his name, his regiment, and a message to his family. They should not bury him, ignorant of his name, in an unidentified grave!

He strove to reach that pencil until his arm fell from exhaustion. No, he could not even write his name and a last message to the loved ones at home!

Then he began to wonder when he would die. Would it be at sunrise to-morrow? Most men did die at sunrise. Would he see the sun rise in another and a better world where there was no suffering, or would he die to-morrow night or the next morning? Then he prayed that, weak and helpless and stranded as he was, the Lord would show him whether there was any way that he could yet be of service to his country.

There was an answer to his prayer. It made every nerve in his body thrill with hope. His door gently opened and out of the darkness came a whisper. "Kunnel!" it said, "I's got nuffin but a jug of cold water for ye! May I come in?"

CHAPTER VIII.

THE UNCONSCIOUS HEROINE.

The mining engineer of 1860 is the colonel of a Federal regiment in 1864. In a single campaign he has left half his regiment on the plains of Virginia, and now in the early autumn he has led its thinned ranks into the valley of Virginia. He has marched his men from Harper's Ferry, by the Charlestown turnpike, over the same route that he rode in 1860, and with the brigade to which his regiment is attached is now in camp at Claremont, one of the farms formerly pointed out to him as the property of Colonel Luke, celebrated for its production of fine horses.

Early one morning he rode out to find the beautiful estate of Audley, which had so impressed him on his first visit. He had some difficulty in recognizing it, although it had fared somewhat better than its neighbors. Its owner was in the service in a distant part of the Confederacy. He found the old servant who had been so polite and hospitable, but who did not now recognize him. He had changed with the estate. His hair could not have been whiter or his aspect more venerable; but his countenance was sorrowful, his clothing worn and rusty. From him the colonel learned that the fine horses and cattle had been exchanged for Confederate securities early in 1861. The wave of invasion and retreat which had so many times rolled up and down the valley had injured Audley less than its neighbors, but it had levelled the fences and destroyed many of its attractions. There was no colored flock of "sassy imps" to greet the traveller. The mistress and the family had left the valley and a general air of sadness pervaded the estate.

The colonel extended his inquiries to the Van Metre farm and mill. Here greater changes had taken place. Its proprietor had brought from the Luray Valley Miss Elizabeth, better known as Miss Betty Keyser, to become its mistress and to bear his name. Then he had enlisted in the Confederate cavalry; her two brothers in other branches of the service. She must have been a young bride, for now in 1864 she had not completed her nineteenth year. Like another Penelope, she was keeping the mill and farm to await her husband's return. There, with Peter, a former slave, Dick Runner, a colored man in the mill, Ginny, his wife, and her young niece of nine years, she still lived, though battles had raged and the unloosed dogs of war with bloody mouths had howled around her for more than three years. The mill farm had suffered with the others. The horses, cattle, all the live-stock, all the wagons and other vehicles, everything which could subsist men or animals had been swept away. The mill was no longer a source of income, for there was no more wheat or corn to be ground. The fences had been levelled; the thrift and prosperity which the traveller witnessed only four years before had melted away in the lurid atmosphere of three years of relentless war.

The brave young wife, with a colored man once a slave but, although now free, faithful to his mistress, had kept the mill and farm through all the disturbances of war. Her husband, after long immunity from wounds and calamities, had been captured, and on his way to Harper's Ferry had been permitted by his captors to call at his home, procure a change of clothing, and take leave of his wife. Then he had been carried North to encounter vicissitudes, of which more will be written in the course of the story. In one respect the reports which the colonel had from his colored informant and other sources agreed. The young wife from the Luray Valley was a woman of strong character who had secured the respect of all who had been brought into contact with her by the fortunes of war; her property had been to some extent protected by Confederates and Unionists, and up to this time even the camp-followers had not raided her home.

When the colonel returned to his camp at Claremont he ordered a guard for the protection of the Van Metre homestead, and directed that it should be maintained until the army moved. Afterward he with other officers of his brigade called at the door and made the young wife's acquaintance. They were all impressed with the brave attempt at cheerfulness which she maintained in her loneliness, and all treated her with deference and kindness; for they knew that as yet she was only a Southern girl, living in the midst of war, at the mercy of those she had been taught to look upon as the deadly enemies of herself and her people, and who were even then holding her husband as a prisoner. She was living, with no companion but her little niece, like so many other sorrowful women North and South, patient in their anxiety and desolation, waiting and praying for peace.

These officers speedily made the discovery that this young Virginia matron was a lady both by nature and education. She expressed her gratitude for their protection of her property, and in every other respect conducted herself with marked propriety and dignity. As already mentioned, it was one of these officers, weary of the eternal sameness of the army ration, who with a tender memory of the superiority of his mother's cooking, one day ventured to ask Mrs. Van Metre whether she would not prepare a meal or two from their supplies. She readily promised to do so, and with some vegetables from her own garden cooked for them a few meals which were long remembered. Thus it happened that upon four or five occasions half a dozen officers of the Vermont brigade and of General Getty's staff broke bread at Mrs. Van Metre's table.

With this sketch in mind we may return to the deserted officer. Early one morning Uncle Dick Runner came to Mrs. Van Metre, with his finger on his lips and an earnest expression of secrecy on his face. "'Fore de Lord, Missus Betty," he whispered, "a Union officer is a dyin' in dat house ober dar whar de Asburys are. I's jes' come from dar and I tink he is dyin' now."

"Why did you not tell me of this before, Dick?" asked his mistress with some severity.

"Why—why—you see, 'twas dis way," he stammered. "Dem Asburys is no good. Dey promis de kunnel's friends to take care of de kunnel. Dey get pay for it. I promis I'd go see when he wanted something. I go dere tree, four times; dem Asburys won't lef me in. Dey say it's none o' my business. Dey goin' to take care ob de kunnel! Early dis morning I steal in de house. I went upstair. De poor man had no water. He can't move. I tink dem Asburys steal his food. I ran got some water. Dat room was an awful place. I clar it up a little, den I come for you."

"Come with me, Dick!" exclaimed the energetic woman, and in a moment she was literally flying over the ground to the house where Bedell lay. Dick followed as fast as his ancient legs would carry him. She walked into the basement without ceremony. "Where is the soldier you are suffering to die in solitude?" she demanded of the miserable couple, who were still living in that part of the house.

"Oh! he's a Lincoln hireling," said the female Asbury. "We don't care for him. We haven't been near him. Who cares if he does die? He's upstairs somewhere!"

"I am ashamed that you are a woman!" exclaimed Mrs. Van Metre. "You promised to take care of him and were paid for it. You stole his food and left him and would not let Dick see him! If he dies you are murderers and ought to be hung!" With this greeting she rushed up to the room where Bedell lay.

"I cannot tell you what I saw or what I said," she afterward explained to the writer. "It was something like this. He lay upon the floor on a straw bed—his eyes sunken and hollow, his great wound where the leg seemed taken off near the hip all exposed, the matter dripping from it. One hand was wrapped in a handkerchief; with the other he was vainly trying to cover himself with an army blanket.

"I was overcome, and instead of going to work

I foolishly asked whether I could do anything for him. The poor fellow burst into tears. 'I hope you will excuse me,' he said. 'I am very weak—I have lost some blood, and it has been lonely here; and when I saw you I thought of my wife—and—and——'

"'Stop!' I said. 'Speaking only weakens you. I see just how it is!' By this time I was quite myself. There was a pail of fresh water which Dick had brought. I gave him a cupful, which he drank, and a second and a third. I said to Dick, 'Take the horse and go for Dr. Osborne. Tell him I want him just as quick as he can come.' Then I dropped on the floor by the poor fellow's side, and with a handkerchief dipped in the cool water washed his face, his hands, his exposed wound. He kept crying and begging my pardon and telling how weak he was. 'Cry!' I said. 'I would cry if I were in your place. Why shouldn't you cry? But you must remember one thing—you are not going to be alone any more. I shall see to that.' So I kept talking and bathing and he crying and thanking me until he seemed quite refreshed. Then I said, 'I do not like to leave you, but I ought to have some things ready when the doctor comes. Are you willing that I should run over to my house and get them?' He said yes quite cheerfully, and I was glad to see that his mind was as clear as mine.

"I went to my house very quickly. Some intuition the day before had led me to boil a chicken, and I set about making a dish of strong broth before the doctor came. Before it was quite ready Dick rode up to my door. He had brought the doctor in half the time I expected. Dick had been sent to see if I had a syringe; if not he was to go to Gaylord for the doctor's. I gave him mine and he took it to Dr. Osborne."

She paused; her animated face became very grave. "I quite forgot myself," she said, "in thinking of what happened almost thirty years ago. You must get the rest of the story from some one else. For me to tell it is too much like blowing my own trumpet."

"Madam," I said, "you ought not to decline to give me the rest of this story. I intend to give it to the world, and I would like to have it from your own lips."

"I am afraid you will not understand me, sir," she said. "I am not entitled to the least credit. Any other woman would have done what I did. Why, the poor man's condition was horrible—horrible!" she exclaimed with a shudder.

"I will assent to anything—I will say that black is white if you wish; but the story—pray go on with the story. You were at the point where the doctor sent for the syringe. Go on and do not stop again!"

"I sent Dick with the syringe. I poured the

broth into a bottle, corked it, and gave it to my niece. I gathered up pieces of linen, two linen sheets, a blanket and a thick comforter, and we both returned to the room where the poor man lay. Dr. Osborne had already removed the officer's coat and vest. He waited while I gave him a cup of the chicken broth. It delighted me to see him drink it and call for more until he had taken the whole. It seemed to put life in him.

"Then the doctor resumed his work, with the assistance of Dick and myself. The details will not interest you. We got him fairly well bathed —his wounds cleansed and in clean bandages. The thick comforter over his straw tick made a softer bed; we placed him between clean sheets with a blanket over him, and before we had quite finished he was asleep."

So much of the story of her first interview with Bedell after he was wounded I had from Mrs. Van Metre's own lips. It was interrupted by the entrance of her husband, whom I then saw for the first time. I was not able afterward to induce her to continue the relation. She could not, she said, talk about herself. I continue the story as I gathered it from other sources.

Bedell continued to sleep so soundly that ordinary conversation did not disturb him. Then the doctor called Mrs. Van Metre to account.

"You are a fine Confederate woman," began the doctor. "Here is a Northern invader, a Lincoln hireling, who has come here to rob us of our property and to conquer us, and you are trying to save his life! Why don't you do your duty and leave him to die?"

"Because a good Confederate—Dr. Osborne—is just as much interested as I am in saving his life; because no true woman could do otherwise than as I am doing. Doctor, let us not have any false pretences between us. When I first came and offered to help him he tried to make me go away; his condition was unfit to be seen, he said. He was thankful, he said, God alone knew how thankful; but he was past all hope. Would I not kindly go away and leave him to die?

"Look at him now," she said as she turned her earnest face toward the man now sleeping so restfully who had been so hopeless only a few hours before. "Are you not repaid already? Can you refuse to help me save his life?"

"Mother Eve was too much for Adam in the first discussion in the garden and you carry too many guns for a country doctor. No! no! God bless your kindly heart, Betty Van Metre! I can refuse you nothing. Friend or enemy, we will save this man if we can!"

"What do you think are his chances, doctor?"

"I can tell much better when he wakes and I can have some conversation with him. I think he has had great distress of mind. But the manner in which he yielded to your influence and his present sleep are very hopeful. He may sleep for hours. Let Uncle Dick go for Ginny. She is an excellent nurse and will watch him as well as you can. Then you go home and we will meet here at four o'clock to-day."

Ginny was sent for and placed in charge. Uncle Dick decided to stay with her, "to keep dem misabul Asburys outen de room." Mrs. Van Metre returned to her own dwelling.

Her restricted larder could still provide a roasted chicken and corn bread made with her own hands for her patient's dinner. She came before the hour. The wounded man was awake, much refreshed by his sleep. But he was still very weak, and when, knowing that he had but one hand, she seated herself on the floor by his bed, carved the chicken, and gave him the delicious and tender meat, he was profuse in his apologies for his nervousness, which still found expression in his moistened eyes. He had made an excellent dinner when the doctor arrived.

Mrs. Van Metre left the room during the doctor's long examination of the patient. At the end of it the doctor said he preferred to talk with her at her own house. Arrangements were made for Ginny to stay with Bedell during the night, and the doctor and Mrs. Van Metre returned to her home.

CHAPTER IX.

THE CONSULTATION—THE COUNTRY DOCTOR—THE DECISION OF THE HEROINE.

"I have had a very satisfactory interview with Lieutenant Bedell," began the doctor. "His mind is clear and I think I can make a good estimate of his chances."

"When can I remove him to my own house, where he can have proper care?" earnestly asked Mrs. Van Metre.

"My dear madam," replied the doctor, "you anticipate me. I do not know that that time will ever come. This man has been very near to death. But for you he would not be living to-day. I would say nothing to discourage you, Heaven knows, but I have studied his condition thoroughly. I suppose you would like to know just what I think his chances are?"

"Most certainly, doctor. But he seemed so much improved to-night that I hoped he was out of danger."

"Very far from that, I assure you. He has a splendid constitution, which gives me all the hope I have. But he has received wounds which in the majority of cases would have been fatal. He has been subjected to fearful surgical operations—then just as nature was asserting herself they tried to move him and he fainted. They carried him back to that room, and there for four days he has lain deserted, the fever and inflammation increasing by neglect and the consciousness of his condition wearing his life away. It is a miracle, almost, that he did not die. Your coming and what you did gave him hope and produced a powerful reaction. But he is very weak. The suppuration of his wounds, now unavoidable, will make heavy drafts upon his vitality, which I tell you frankly I do not believe he can endure. As for moving him now, that is out of the question. He would die before you got him out of the house!"

"Poor fellow! and he has a wife and children! And how brave he is! and how grateful! Must he die? Don't give him up, doctor! Is there nothing we can do to save him?"

"My dear madam, I have never felt our poverty and destitution as I do to-day. Yes, something might be done for him. If we had stimulants and medicines to brace him up and enable him to meet the drafts which his wounds will make upon his system, his superb constitution might pull him through. If we had the quinine and whiskey left by his friends and which have been stolen from his bed, they would do much."

"Cannot we buy these stimulants with money?"

"No. The only stimulant to be had is a quart or so of cider brandy from an illicit still. It burns like nitric acid—it is not as good for our purposes as alcohol. As for quinine, I have not seen an ounce of it in a year."

"But, doctor, don't tell me that it is impossible to get what will save such a life! There must be some place where it exists and some way to get it!"

"There is at Harper's Ferry a depot of the Sanitary Commission, where there is an abundance of everything we want, but those supplies are for the Federal army, not for us Confederates. They are as safe from you and me as if they were locked behind bolts and bars and guarded by an angel with a flaming sword!"

"Do you say, doctor, that if you had those medicines from Harper's Ferry you believe you could save the life of that wounded officer?"

"I do most certainly believe I could," said the doctor with an earnestness that was very grave.

His auditor started from her seat. She walked quickly to the window and looked at the setting sun. Then she walked back and stood before the medical man like a statue. There was a ring of determination in her voice which thrilled him.

"Doctor," she said, "prepare me a list of the things you need, and which you think the Sanitary Commission can furnish. To-morrow I shall go to Harper's Ferry and get them!"

The doctor's breath was almost taken away. After a little he managed to exclaim: "My dear woman, what are you thinking about? Have you gone crazy? Don't you know that Harper's Ferry is in the hands of our enemies? You could not get within their lines! If you could, they would arrest and probably hang you as a spy. Positively it is the most reckless proposition I ever heard in my life. I cannot let you do it!"

"But I must do it, doctor! There is no one else to go. We must have the medicines and I have no choice."

"Why do you take so much interest in this Northern man who has been wounded in battle by our own friends?"

"I am not surprised that you ask, and I do not know that I can answer your question to your satisfaction or, indeed, to my own. He is a wounded, suffering man, with a home far away, and in it are a wife and children. If any woman knowing that and seeing him as I have seen him could do otherwise than I have done, she is not such a woman as I am. Then weeks ago his general placed guards upon and protected my home. From all his brother-officers myself and my little niece have received the most courteous and considerate treatment. This officer and others have eaten at my table. I cannot help thinking that I should be doing a good deed if I could help save such a noble man!

"But my strongest reason is yet to be given. You may laugh at me and think me superstitious if you like. But when Dick Runner first told me that a Union officer was dying in that house, the thought possessed me that if I could help that man, some Northern woman might help my husband. This notion, if you will call it such, absolutely controls me. When I go forward something tells me that I am doing right. When I hold back and ask why I should take any trouble for him, I can almost hear a voice saying, 'Betty Van Metre, as you deal with that suffering man so shall your husband be dealt with. Nurse him, cure him, do all in your power for him, if you wish ever again to see your husband!' I feel, I know that in some way the fate of my husband is bound up with that of this Union officer!

"Am I not doing right, doctor? Here I am alone, inexperienced, and not yet twenty years old. If I am doing wrong you, who have had experience, ought to advise me. I am acting according to my lights."

"Mrs. Van Metre, you have answered me. I do solemnly believe you are acting the part of à true woman. If you were my daughter I would tell you so. But I cannot advise you to go to

Harper's Ferry. The turnpike is beset with tramps and guerillas. The prospect of success is too remote, and I believe you will fail."

"I might succeed where a man would fail. I shall go to-morrow morning, so you had better make all your preparations and give me full directions!"

"I must at least insist on your postponing it another day. I ought to consider you an obstinate, wilful child. You will be insulted, mortified, probably imprisoned, and you will fail. Yet I shall probably let you go, the man will die, and I shall never see you again!"

"You are not an encouraging adviser, doctor. But I am in the hands of the Almighty. I must trust him and do what seems to be necessary. It will take Peter a day to repair the old wagon, so we have that time for preparation."

She again visited her patient and prepared him for the night. He was cheerful, thankful, but her heart sank when she found how little strength he had. She arranged with the three colored servants to see that he was not again left alone.

The next was a busy day. From her own nearly exhausted larder, the box of crackers, and the milk of a neighbor's cow she provided his food for the next day. He saw that preparations were being made for something and he wished to know what. She made some excuse, which satisfied him.

Successive Confederate and Union invasions of the valley had swept from her farm every horse save one—an old animal, spavined, foundered, worthless for almost every purpose. A long-disused wagon had also been left because it would scarcely hold together to be moved away. Uncle Peter, who was a skilful cobbler of wheeled vehicles as well as shoes, was directed out of the remains to reconstruct a wagon which should withstand the hard usage of a journey to Harper's Ferry and back, a distance of more than forty miles, over roads which had not been repaired since the beginning of the war and which had been many times furrowed by army wagons and artillery. This work occupied him for the day.

As soon as the doctor called in the morning his patient insisted upon being informed of the preparations going on and what they signified. "I will tell you," said the doctor, "and then I must rely upon your discretion. You must promise not to attempt to dissuade Mrs. Van Metre from what she intends to do. She insists upon making an attempt to procure from Harper's Ferry the stimulants which you must have if you are to recover.

"I think the journey a most dangerous one. I do not think she will be allowed to enter the town. If she gets to the Sanitary depot I do not believe she will be given the articles we need.

But she is so determined that I dare not take the responsibility of preventing her, nor should you. On the contrary, I think we should encourage and assist her."

Bedell assented; in fact, he was almost too feeble to resist. In the evening Mrs. Van Metre took the control of the sick-room. Ginny, the colored nurse, was to remain with the officer, and in her possession was placed the most nourishing food which Mrs. Van Metre's stores could supply. Then they bathed the hands, face, and much of the body of the wounded man, with such a comforting effect that he went to sleep under their hands.

Our heroine very much wanted something from Bedell which would serve her for credentials, otherwise the only proof that he was alive and that she was acting for him was her own word. But he was too weak to write or even to give her instructions which would be useful. The army had moved and he did not know that he had an acquaintance in the town.

Under these circumstances she felt at liberty to examine Bedell's clothing to see whether she could not find something that would prove his identity. In one of the pockets of his coat she found a letter; the stamp of the War Office was upon the envelope. She removed the letter from the envelope and found that its folds adhered together. It had been saturated by his blood.

Carefully separating one of these folds, she saw that the letter was the official announcement of his last promotion, directed with his full name. She thrust it into her bosom, gave to Ginny her last directions, breathed a prayer for the safety of her patient, and about midnight returned to her own home.

CHAPTER X.

THE FIRST EXPEDITION TO HARPER'S FERRY.

Early the next morning Mistress Betty took her seat in the rickety vehicle and slowly started her stiffened Rosinante on his twenty-mile journey to Harper's Ferry and return. It could not be said that she handled the ribbons gracefully, for in her case the cord of a dismantled bedstead replaced the reins. She encountered parties of camp-followers and tramps, but none of them could discover any reward for robbery in her empty conveyance. The road was rough and her progress slow. It was seven long hours after she started before she reached the pickets of the Union post.

To the young officer in command of the picket she told the plain truth. She gave her true name—said she lived in Berryville, that her husband and brothers were in the Confederate army, that she was a Southern woman. She said that near her home in Berryville, in a vacant house, there was an officer of the Union army desperately wounded and about to die for want of nourishing food and stimulating remedies.

She gave his name and regiment. She had come, she said, to procure these necessaries from the Sanitary Commission. She had no other errand. She asked to be taken before the general in command of the post without delay, that she might accomplish her errand and return.

It was about this time that smuggling into the Confederacy was at its height. The notorious Belle Boyd had been detected and imprisoned, and many other agents and spies had not only carried medicines and mails, but the Union plans to the Southern leaders. These operations had been the cause of the loss of many lives and much Union property. The greatest strictness now prevailed. No one was permitted to pass the lines without orders from the general commanding the army in that military department.

The officer of the picket feared that he had one of these spies in petticoats on his hands, and yet, being a gentleman, he could not withhold his confidence from that frank, open face or order a search of her person, to which she volunteered to submit. It was the hour for the relief of his guard, and riding by her side he escorted the singular conveyance and its driver to the quarters of General Stevenson, to whom, while she waited without, the young officer told her story. It elicited many oh's and ah's and other expressions of incredulity from the experienced veteran.

Then the driver was called into the general's presence and sharply questioned. She repeated her story. She had no other, and there was not a fact or circumstance in it upon which the general could hang the shadow of a suspicion.

Her bearing was so unassuming, her story so absolutely unexceptionable, that the general was annoyed because he could not take exception to either. He took refuge in fuming and fault-finding. "Why can't you women stay at home and attend to your own affairs?" he growled. "I would have much preferred to do so," she said, "but if I had your officer would surely have died." "There it is again!" he said. "They always have some reason on their lips that the devil himself can't answer. Now if this was a man I'd know what to do with him. Probably I would hang him as a spy! It is easier to deal with fifty men than one soft-spoken woman. Here you, madam! Don't you know that this yarn of yours is the d—dest improbable story ever invented? Excuse me for swearing in the presence of a lady, for you look like a lady and d—n me if I don't believe you are a lady. But why didn't you bring a letter from the officer when you were going on such a dangerous errand where you would inevitably risk your life?"

"The lieutenant was too feeble to write, sir, and his right hand is all shot to pieces. He would have made the effort if I had asked him, but I knew he could not write, and the exertion would have made him weaker!"

"But a woman as bright as you are might have brought some credentials—a button from his coat or something from his pocket. How can I take your unconfirmed story?"

"While he was asleep, sir, I confess I did examine his pockets, and in one of them I found this." Dexterously opening a seam in her skirt, she extracted from it the blood-stained letter, which she handed to the general, who passed it to a member of his staff and directed him to read it. The officer removed the letter from its envelope without glancing at the direction. While separating the adhering folds he saw its beginning.

"Bedell! Bedell!" exclaimed the officer. "How came you by this, madam? Bedell was in our brigade. He was mortally wounded and died more than a week ago. We had to leave him, poor fellow, and it was a shame that we did so. I know he is dead, for the nurse we left with him came into camp the next day and reported that he died during the night. This letter must have been taken from his body."

"Lieutenant Bedell was not dead this morning at sunrise," she said, and her voice was very tender as she continued: "He would have been in my house, but he was too weak to be moved. I left him in a deserted house near mine in charge of a faithful old colored couple. His hand is shot and useless; he has not strength to hold a pen. He will die if I do not get what I came for. I fear he will die before I get home. My own doctor has said so. That is why I came, gentlemen," she continued. "Pray think of one of your wives or daughters on my errand, and for their sakes give me what I came for and let me go. I do not ask for myself, but for your brother-officer, now very near his end. I am trying to save him for his own wife and children. I am afraid if I am much longer delayed I shall not find him alive when I go home."

Her lips and her voice were tremulous as she closed her pathetic appeal. No one answered her. There were eyes in the group that were not dry, and the veteran general seemed to be trying to divert attention from his own emotions by vehemently blowing his nose. Just then, unannounced, another officer entered the room. "I hear there is a lady here whom I want to see," he exclaimed, and rushing forward he strode up to the timid woman and warmly grasped both her hands. "God bless you, Mrs. Van Metre!" he exclaimed. "Why are you here and what can this camp do for you?" Then she recognized in his cordial greeting and earnest look the voice and face of one of the officers who had sat at her table and partaken of the luxuries of her cookery. "Tell me," he repeated, "what any of us can do for you."

"You can do me a very great favor if you can convince these gentlemen that I am telling the truth," she said. "I am not here for myself, but for one of your brother-officers, Lieutenant Bedell."

"Poor Bedell!" he responded. "How shameful it was that we left him to die. I should have stayed with him at any risk, although he insisted that we should leave him for our duties with the army. But he did not suffer long. The nurse whom we left with him reported that he died the next morning. But pray what can be done for him now?"

"Lieutenant Bedell is not dead, as I have assured these gentlemen," said Mrs. Van Metre. "We still hope, Dr. Osborne and myself, that we can save him, if I can have the things for which I have come."

"You can have anything that this camp can furnish for such a purpose, but the news is too good. Bedell alive! I could as readily have believed he was raised from the dead," warmly responded the officer. "But what do you want? What have you come for? You shall have it at once!"

The general here interposed, and turning to the messenger asked:

"Are you a Union woman?"

"I am not," she replied. "I am a Southern woman to the last drop of my blood. My husband and brothers are Confederate soldiers and my husband is now in the hands of your people a prisoner of war. I hope and pray that the South may yet be victorious and your Northern army defeated."

"Rebel or not, you are a brave and I believe you are a good, true woman!" said the general. "But about giving you supplies which may be used to cure some sick Confederate! we shall have to think about that. What shall we do with her, gentlemen? Her conduct violates all the rules of war. I suppose it is my duty to arrest and imprison her as a spy. I wish she had not come. I fear she will prove an elephant on our hands. How we should be laughed at if we gave her what she wants and the supplies went straight to Mosby's camp! Again I ask, what shall we do with her?"

"I would like to ask the lady why she takes so much interest in the fate of an enemy?" asked a young officer.

"Dr. Osborne, my physician, asked me that question and I have asked it of myself. I do not know that I can give a satisfactory answer. Lieutenant Bedell and his brother-officers placed guards over my little property—they have all treated me with the courtesy of gentlemen. My husband is a prisoner. I have thought that if I could save the life of this man for his wife and family, the Lord might put it into the heart of some Northern woman to be equally kind and helpful to my husband. If these suggestions do not answer you, then I say that I suppose it is because I am a woman and have a woman's heart, and I cannot—Heaven knows I cannot—see such a brave man suffer and die without doing all that I can to save him. If these reasons are not sufficient I am sorry—I can only say that I have no other."

"If she is not a trustworthy woman there never was one," said the officer who had previously made her acquaintance. "I would believe her as I would my mother. Then are we not bound to take some risk for Bedell? I vote for furnishing her with everything she wants, and I am ready to take the whole risk!"

"I think, gentlemen, we are all agreed," said the general with the caution of an army officer. "We believe what this lady says. She is working for the life of one of our brother-officers. We will furnish her with all the materials and facilities which will promote her good work. If any one entertains a different opinion, now is his time to express it."

There was no dissension. All set about contributing to the work. Every possible attention was shown to Mrs. Van Metre. Even the old horse was refreshed with such a feed as he had not enjoyed since the war began.

Mrs. Van Metre gave them the memorandum

prepared by Dr. Osborne of Bedell's real necessities. To this the surgeons and agents of the Commission made liberal additions. The Sanitary and Christian Commissions, the stores and private supplies of the officers were drawn upon, and the load as made up severely taxed the strength and capacity of the vehicle. The driver decided that it would be unsafe to undertake the transportation of such a load in the day-time through a region so destitute, infested by so many bands of roving robbers, all following their merciless instincts. The supplies were closely packed in boxes and the return postponed until evening, notwithstanding one of the officers very significantly suggested that she would run no risk of attack on her return.

At nightfall she left the camp followed by the God-speed of officers and men, her heart as full of gratitude as her wagon was with medicines and necessaries. The old horse appeared to have renewed his youth and activity. He picked his way cautiously over the rough places, and wherever he came to a smoother road, without a word or touch of the whip he bowled along at a pace of six or seven miles an hour.

Her heart sank once on the return journey. She was within two miles of her home when she heard the sound of horses galloping on the road behind her. The old horse increased his paces, but she knew she was being rapidly overtaken.

They must be her pursuers, she thought—they were guerillas or robbers. It was too much that after all her success she should lose her supplies when so near her home—that her good fortune should desert her and her enterprise come to naught!

No! no! Thank Heaven! Separating into two lines, the party swept past her. The leader spoke. She recognized the voice of her acquaintance who had been so kind to her during the day. It was expressed in different language, but it filled her agitated breast with the same feeling which gave strength to the arms and firmness to the hearts of the disciples when, toiling at the oars, they heard through storm and tempest the cheering message, "It is I, be not afraid!" The voice of this leader said, "No guerillas—no robbers will harm you. We are your escort to Berryville!"

Her escort waited at the junction of the road leading to her home with the turnpike, and watched her until she reached her own door. As she drove past them they gave her a respectful fusillade of good wishes and kind messages to her patient. She found the doctor waiting for her, much troubled by the delay of her return. The lieutenant was sleeping under the watchful eye of Ginny, but he had been growing weaker during the day. The abundant load of supplies was transferred to Mrs. Van Metre's store-room, where it was safe under lock and key. But the doctor would not defer the administration of a remedy from which he expected immediate results. He prepared it, and with the fortunate messenger went to the patient's bedside, aroused and administered it to him.

CHAPTER XI.

THE PECULIARITIES OF THE COUNTRY DOCTOR— THE REMOVAL AND CONCEALMENT UNDER DIFFICULTIES OF A STALWART ENEMY.

UPON several occasions in my life it has happened to me to be brought into contact with the country doctor. I have met him socially and professionally, and in one instance he has been closely connected with my own family. I have always found him exhibiting the same specific characters. As an interesting species of our race, he deserves some description.

He is, I believe, the most charitable and kind-hearted expression of our humanity. His life is laborious—he belongs to the most arduous and difficult of what are known as the learned professions. He deals with the complex mechanism of life, which is never at rest, is in constant operation, and through our negligence of its demands, exposed to disarrangement and injury. Unless he understands all its delicate functions he is useless, and the knowledge of these functions is only to be acquired by long and patient study. He must be able to detect the diseased parts, not by simple inspection, as in the case of other machinery, but by symptoms, deductions, or by what is called diagnosis, and when he has located the defect he must know how it can be repaired. To practise at all and to protect himself against the perils of malpractice, he must attain to a measure of skill only to be acquired by a long and thorough course of training.

When he has acquired the knowledge necessary to his being admitted to his profession, he cannot, like the ordinary mechanic, sit in his shop and have his work brought to him to be done at his leisure, where his tools are ready to his hand. No. Nature cannot wait—pain, her messenger, is imperative. The country doctor must be ready to answer her call at any hour of the day or night. More often than otherwise he will be aroused from his refreshing sleep at midnight—he will have to harness his own horse and in storm and darkness make his way over hill and mountain to some distant cottage where the patient lies impatiently awaiting his coming.

Is he always adequately rewarded? Does he stipulate for and secure his fee in advance? No! In the majority of cases he performs his service upon a credit which will only mature in another world. It is none the less valuable on that account, for he never stops to inquire whether the patient is able to pay. The city practitioner called from his sleep in the night by a stranger may coolly refer the messenger to his young partner at some number a dozen blocks away and shut the door in his face. The country doctor is never guilty of such unfeeling incivility. He answers the call in person. Wherefore it is that throughout my professional life I have thought and said of the country doctor, "He is the true Samaritan, an honor to his profession and to mankind."

As Adam Smith once wrote of humanity, these country doctors are very much alike—very uniform. Why did not Dr. Osborne, when he was sent for in great haste by Mrs. Van Metre, stop and inquire whether the patient was not "a Lincoln hireling"? He was a Confederate, was Dr. Osborne. Politically, he was more interested in killing than in curing the officers of the Northern army. Why at least did he not stop and ascertain whether the patient would promise to compensate him if he recovered and should ever have the pecuniary ability to do so? Why did he come at the first summons, take a deep interest in the case, repeat his visits from day to day, and never omit them until Bedell had no further need of him, without so much as one word on the subject of his fees? It was because he was a country doctor!

Dr. Osborne is dead. The writer has recently been among the people in the region where he lived and died. There is no question about the

PECULIARITIES OF THE COUNTRY DOCTOR. 99

esteem in which he was held by that community. When its members answered the writer's inquiries about him their voices were low, their accents affectionate, their testimony unanimous that he was a good man.

Although the exigencies of war had for a long time deprived his patients of their benefits, Dr. Osborne thoroughly understood the practical use of all modern surgical instruments and of all the medical remedies described in the Pharmacopœia. He was simply amazed at the success of Mrs. Van Metre's expedition. The agents of the Sanitary and Christian Commissions had not only furnished all the articles mentioned in his written memorandum, but having obtained from the faithful messenger a description of Bedell's condition, they had added such things as they thought might prove useful in his case. The doctor left the coffee and tea, the canned meats, vegetables, and other food supplies to the administration of Mrs. Van Metre. Those which belonged to his own profession he displayed upon one of her tables. First of all, from the requisite materials he compounded the strengthening and stimulating mixture which was to be administered every two hours. The draught of the previous evening had arrested the weakening process, and the first application in the morning appeared to turn the face of his patient in the direction of recovery.

Then how the good doctor did revel in the

pleasures of his profession and thank God for the liberality of the Sanitary Commission. For this mountaineer was a man of experience and learning, and he knew the uses of all the medicines and instruments, many of which he had seldom seen during the recent years of war. With a touch of affection he proceeded to remove the coverings and arrange the medicines in order. His heart leaped in his bosom when he came to the instruments. For his brother-surgeons had sent him a very complete assortment of the most modern and approved manufactures, with a grateful note requesting his acceptance of them after his patient had been cured. He laid them out, one by one, upon the table, surveyed and rejoiced over them, more pleased than a queen by the presentation of a casket of jewels.

As soon as the patient had begun to feel the strengthening effects of the new remedies, he was visited by the doctor, Mrs. Van Metre, and the colored couple, Dick and Ginny. They trespassed upon the Asburys' fire enough to heat a quantity of water. The old dressings of his wounds were softened, removed, and committed to the flames, and new, clean bandages were applied. His entire body was thoroughly bathed. Uncle Dick was a very fair barber. He trimmed the patient's hair and whiskers and even attempted a moderate shampoo. Clean linen was put upon him, the cot bedstead and mattress from the Ferry were set up, and the patient was placed between clean sheets upon them. Even the naked room was made a little more attractive and less desolate.

Bedell bore the fatigue of this change fairly well, and the doctor left him with the hope that if no set-back occurred his removal might be attempted within the next three or four days.

The house where the officer lay was a good third of a mile from the Van Metre homestead, where Peter Dennis and near which Dick and Ginny lived. It was not safe to leave the lieutenant alone. "Dem Asburys," as Uncle Dick persisted in calling them, were unsafe neighbors, almost as dangerous as the guerillas and camp-followers. Mrs. Van Metre did not wish to leave her little niece alone in the house, and although the colored neighbors would stay with the wounded man during the night, Mrs. Van Metre experienced considerable difficulty in arranging matters during the day. She finally compromised by going to her patient once in three hours, keeping up his courage by a few minutes of cheerful conversation, and then returning home.

But this plan involved much labor and left both places exposed during her temporary absence. She therefore determined as soon as Bedell's strength would permit that he should be removed to her own home, where he could have cheerful companionship and not be subject to exposure.

How was this removal to be effected? He was a heavy man, he could not yet stand upon his single leg, he was in the second story of the house, and except her colored servants she had no one to assist her. She called upon Dick Runner to devise some means for his transfer.

"Dick," she said, "the wounded soldier must not be left in that solitary, exposed house any longer. I want him removed to my house. It must be done at once—to-day—and you must find a way to do it."

"Dat's a hard job, Missus Betty! De kunnel can't walk—he mus' be carried. He's berry heavy. I don't see how it's to be done."

"But you must see. It's cruel to have him lie there and suffer when he could be so comfortable with us. We must move him to-day and you must find the way!"

"I'll do the best I can, but you mus' give me time to tink! You are allus in a drefful hurry, Miss Betty. You kinder scares me." So saying he seated himself upon a bowlder, clasped his head with both hands, and was apparently buried deep in reflection.

He did not keep her waiting long. "Miss Betty," he exclaimed, "I's got it—I's got it! But we mus' not move him to-day. Dem Asburys is a-watchin'. They has been four or five tramps hazin' round here and dey specks something. Up in the garret of the mill there is an old stretcher; dey carried stones and bricks on it. I knows I kin find it. You wait till night, put his mattress an' comforter on it, Ginny an' I will carry one end, Peter an' some other darky will take the other, an' we'll carry him right over to your house!"

She recognized the wisdom of waiting until evening, and Dick was directed to prepare the stretcher and engage the carriers. The only opposition came from Bedell. He would not, he said, helpless hulk that he was, be carried into her house to turn it into a hospital. He was grateful enough to her, Heaven knew, but this was too much. He was beginning to have some hope—he was getting stronger. She must let him fight out the battle where he was, alone.

"Lieutenant," said the determined woman, "you are not going to waste your strength nor my time. I am stronger than you are and my three servants will help me. You are going over to my house to-night, and your objections will not weigh a feather's weight. You are a sick man—you don't know what is best for you. I do! Here comes Ginny with your coffee and a ration of canned beef. That is good for you beyond any controversy! Now be good and obedient and obey your nurse!"

Bedell was silenced. He obeyed. That night the old stretcher was brought, the heavy man was laid upon it, and three colored men and

Ginny carried him gently down the stairs out under the open sky. It was raining. The Virginia woman protected the Union officer from the rain with her umbrella—the procession moved slowly, though safely, across the fields to her home.

Mrs. Van Metre had asked him whether he had not been refreshed by the sponge-bath given him by Dr. Osborne, and he had responded with great enthusiasm. She thereupon directed Dick and Ginny, in spite of his remonstrances, to repeat the process. After it was completed he was placed in a broad, soft bed in a pleasantly furnished apartment, which he afterward learned was the room of his hostess, which she had surrendered for his use. Then she gave him a cooling, quieting draught, prepared by the doctor, which seemed to take away from him all disposition to resist, and he slept.

His hostess was as much relieved from anxiety as himself. He was removed without the knowledge of any one but herself and her trusted servants. Tramps and guerillas would scarcely suspect his presence in her own room. She might reasonably hope that he would be permitted to travel the road to convalescence and recovery without interference or interruption. However, his greatest danger lay in the possibility of discovery, and to prevent that should be the study of her present life.

CHAPTER XII.

THE DREAM WHICH WAS NOT ALL A DREAM.

THE journey to Harper's Ferry, the anxiety and excitement, which were constant until the wounded man was safe under her own roof, would have worn out any one who was not sustained by a strong sense of duty. Mas. Vsn Metre had determined to nurse him through that first night in his new quarters and had dismissed her colored assistants to their homes. When she saw how peacefully her patient was sleeping, she experienced a strong desire herself for a similar rest. She extinguished all the lights, dropped upon a lounge, threw a shawl over herself, and was soon sleeping as refreshingly as her charge.

Both slept far into the long autumn night. The lieutenant first awoke. His slight movement showed him that his nurse was at her post of duty.

"Do you want anything?" she asked as she started to relight the lamps

"Please do not strike a light," he said. "Leave the room as it is. I wish to tell you something. If I saw your face I might not have the courage to tell you what I wish to say. Will you kindly sit where I can feel your presence?"

She seated herself by his bedside and took his unwounded hand. She waited some time in silence and then asked:

"What was it that you wished to say?"

"Mrs. Van Metre," he said in a low but very firm voice, "I have seen your husband to-night."

She was startled. She thought he had suddenly been stricken with insanity. "How did you know that I had a husband?" she asked.

"I do not know unless I dreamed it," he said, and again relapsed into silence.

"Tell me the story," she said. "There is no one to hear it but ourselves."

"It was a dream," he said. "I know it was a dream. There is no truth in dreams. It is absurd to tell them, yet this one was fearfully real. You will not think me light-headed or that I have lost my senses?"

"Indeed I will not. You excite my curiosity. I should much like to hear it. I am curious to learn how you came to know about my husband. These dreams have sometimes proved prophetic."

"If I shall not earn your contempt I will tell you the whole story. I fear my sleep has weakened me, and I may never be stronger."

"Tell it in your own way. We can discuss it afterward."

"This was the way of it. I was in that horrible room where you found me and I was dying of thirst and starvation. What I wanted more than anything else was to write my name, regiment, the date of my death, and the place where I was to be buried. I wanted my wife and friends to know where I lay. It appeared that I had already suffered all that mortal man could suffer and live. With great pains I had found a pencil and a piece of board upon which I was trying to write my name. The Asburys had been watching me with hungry eyes. They seized the board and tore it from me. In the struggle I lost consciousness.

"Then I was restored far enough to know that some one gave me a refreshing drink. In an instant I was another being—all my pains, cares, anxieties had vanished. I was as light as air. By a gentle spring with my one limb I could ascend indefinitely—to the heavens if I wished. I was supremely happy. I pitied those who were tied down to this dull, senseless earth. Distance was nothing to me. A wish transported me anywhere I chose to go. I wanted to see my home. By a graceful series of ascents and descents, like travelling over a rolling country, I was there. My children were hanging on my neck, my wife was embracing me and saying: 'It was cruel of you, Henry, not to write us for all these long weeks when we were mourning you as dead, and then come upon us so suddenly. Your own colonel reported you as mortally wounded and then as dead, and we never expected to see you again.'

"'I have been wounded and very near to death,' I said. 'Do you not see that it is only a part of your husband who has come back to you? But for a woman as good and true as yourself I should have died as awful a death as you could imagine, and you never would have known where I was buried.' Then I told her all about you—how energetic and kind you had been, and how you had saved my life when you were in great trouble yourself. I told her of your anxiety about your husband, who was a prisoner if he was alive, and that you sometimes feared he was not living, and that I owed you such a debt of gratitude that I ought to find your husband and get him released if he was in prison, for you had saved me and given me back to her. 'God bless her!' exclaimed my wife. 'Our children shall be taught to love her and I will never make a prayer that does not invoke blessings on her head.' Then we went into our children's room, and I heard them talking in their sleep of their father.

"My wife was suddenly startled. I had tried already to call her attention to my crippled condition, but her mind was so full of joy that she did not notice what I said. Now she saw my defect. 'Why, Henry,' she exclaimed, 'you have lost a part of yourself!'

"'You were too proud of the strength and

activity of your husband. So was I. It was necessary that our pride should have a fall. I have lost my leg, but as I said before I have gained the friendship of a woman who is as noble and good and kind as yourself. Could I say more of any woman?'

"Just here comes in the remarkable part of my dream, You must think me foolish for relating it to you. But it did seem so real!"

"Indeed, you misjudge me," said his auditor. "Your strange vision interests me. Perhaps I will tell you how deeply when you have finished. I should be sorry if you did not give me the whole of the story."

"My dear wife whispered in my ear that she feared I had been ungrateful. 'I am strangely drawn toward that woman,' she said. 'Think how great a debt we owe her! What is her name? Where did you leave her? Is she happy? She cannot possibly be contented not knowing the fate of her husband. It would be hard for us to part with you again, but we would do it for you to go back to her and help her find her husband.'

"'You recall me to my duty,' I said. 'I do not know why I left her. She is in trouble. Nothing but the sorrow that strains the heart to the point of breaking could have impressed the sadness which was in her face when I last saw it. I deserve to be punished for leaving her. I have been ungrateful. I will go back to her and do what I can to repair my error.'

"I remember that my wife stood before me, and I thought I never saw a woman with a more noble expression upon her face. 'Henry,' she said, 'I have been very proud of you. But if you can rest until you have either aided that woman to find her husband or to ascertain that he is no longer living, you are not the man I married— you are no husband of mine!'

"Then, as if a curtain had been let down from the sky before me, I seemed to be shut out from my wife and my home. Next, by one of those mysterious changes which I cannot even try to explain, I was in a camp of many thousand Confederate prisoners—soldiers of the Southern army. There was a long building of one story over which floated a hospital flag. Near it, shaded by large trees, were tents in which very sick men lay. In one of them there was only a single patient. He lay upon a cot, to which he had just been brought. He was dreadfully emaciated. His head had just been shaved, his body had been washed, and as he lay upon his back, his hollow cheeks, sunken eyes, and ashen face showed that he had been a great sufferer, probably from a long fever. He could only speak in whispers. An old gray-haired general with a benignant face, a lady young enough to be his daughter, a surgeon, and an old colored man stood around the sick man. The lady had turned her face away from the sufferer; her breast was swelling with emotion and her gentle eyes were filled with tears.

"In a corner of the tent stood another person. He had a fawning, treacherous, hang-dog look. I have no words adequate to describe the villanous meanness of his appearance or expression. A soldier stood beside him who appeared to be his guard.

"'What do you make of his case, doctor?' I heard the general ask.

"'It is a case of brain fever complicated with the most inexcusable negligence and I fear with violence. Look at his wrists—they carry the marks of manacles which have worn away the skin.'

"'He was very violent, sir. He was dangerous. He tried to kill me. We had to restrain him or he would have killed us all,' whined the wretch who stood by the soldier.

"'Silence, you villain! Not another word from your lying lips!' said the general, with a most righteous ring to his voice. Then I saw that the man addressed was a rat-mouthed, ferret-eyed caitiff in the dress of a nurse or hospital attendant. He seemed crushed by the words of the general.

"'Can you save the poor man's life?' asked the general of the surgeon.

"'I do not know—I cannot answer now. His case is very doubtful. The fever is still upon him. We have been very gentle in our treatment of him. If he does not sink under it I shall have some hope. It was most fortunate that your daughter found him this morning. Another access of his fever would inevitably have been fatal.'

"'Was it not cruel to shave his head in that manner? Why was it necessary, doctor?' inquired the sweet voice of the lady.

"'The answer is scarcely fitting for a lady's ear,' replied the surgeon. 'It was not only necessary, it was indispensable. He would otherwise have been devoured by vermin!'

"'He wouldn't let me do anything. He wouldn't take anything from me,' began the wretch.

"'I tell you silence!' thundered the general. He called in a sergeant and a file of men. 'Take that man,' he said, pointing to the miserable creature who had just spoken, 'to the guard-house. Put him in irons. Give him bread and water only. If this poor prisoner dies his life shall pay the forfeit, if I take it with my own hands.'

"Then the sufferer on the cot made an effort to speak. We could all hear him, for there was no sound to break the silence but the sighs of the compassionate woman. 'Will some one write to my wife in the valley,' he said, 'and tell her where I am? I know that my letters have been suppressed. She has not heard from me for many weeks. She must think I am dead!'

"'What is the name and post-office address of your wife?' asked the general.

"'Her name is Betty Van Metre and she lives in Berryville, in the valley,' said the sick man.

"I had hitherto said not a word. But when I heard your name and knew that the patient was your husband I could not restrain myself. 'What is the name of this place?' I asked. 'Gentlemen, I know this man's wife. Tell me the name of this place, and she shall be here as quick as steam and the railroad can bring her. I owe my life to Mrs. Van Metre!'

"All except the lady stared at me as if I was an impertinent intruder. The general demanded by what right I thrust myself into their councils in a matter which did not concern me.

"I tried to remonstrate. I told them that if they knew how much I owed to you they would not stand upon ceremony. I said, 'For the sake of that poor sick man, for mine—as you hope for blessings here and for mercy hereafter, tell me the name of this place, and I will thank you on my knees.'"

"Did you learn the name of the place?"

"Alas! no. The earnestness of my appeal—my intense anxiety awoke me. The vision passed and I heard your voice almost at my side."

"Are you quite certain that the man who lay upon the cot gave my name?"

"As certain as that I now hear your voice."

"Would you recognize the face of the sick man if you saw it in a picture?"

"I think so—I have no doubt I should."

Mrs. Van Metre controlled her feelings more perfectly than the wounded officer. "I heard in May last," she said, "that my husband had been captured a second time near Spottsylvania Court House. Up to that time he had been a faithful correspondent. Since then I have heard nothing from him. I cannot understand his silence. I think I should have died of grief if I had not kept my mind employed. Your vision, as you call it, at least suggests the chance that he may be alive. I had almost lost hope in these days of weary suspense and waiting."

"Your husband is alive. He is in good hands now, although he has been a sufferer from some treachery. You will see him again. I wanted to live before for my country, children, and my wife. I have now another reason, for if I live I will find your husband and give him back to you!"

Mrs. Van Metre now drew the curtains, for the sun was already reddening the crest of the eastern Blue Ridge. She took from a drawer a photograph album containing a number of portraits. She held it before his eyes and began to turn the leaves. At the second portrait he said:

"Stop! That is the face of the man I saw last night on the cot in the hospital tent. He was not stalwart and vigorous as he appears here, but it is the same face, worn and wasted by fever and exposure."

"That picture," said Mrs. Van Metre, "is the last photograph of my husband."

There was silence in the room during the long morning twilight while the darkness of the night was slowly changing to the bright light of day. "I am sincerely grateful for your interest," she said, "but you are excited now, and in your weak condition excitement is dangerous. It is very singular that the events of the last few days should have so multiplied your chances of recovery and so filled my heart with confidence and hope. It is said that dreams are only baseless imaginations. That may be true. Nevertheless yours has been very comforting, a healing balm for at least one wounded heart. A very great and good man, troubled as we have been, had his life changed by a supernatural revelation. Standing before a great king, he declared that 'he was not disobedient to the heavenly vision.' It will make me stronger, a more hopeful wife, and a more earnest woman to believe that my husband lives and that through you I may yet see his face."

CHAPTER XIII.

THE BATTLE OF OPEQUAN OR WINCHESTER—THE PROGRESS OF THE WOUNDED OFFICER—THE SKILL AND ENTERPRISE OF HIS HOSTESS.

Hopeless, in his desolate room, waiting for death, Bedell had heard the guns of Sheridan's first great battle in the valley. It was fought on the 19th of September. The Unionists call it the battle of the Opequan; the Confederates, with more propriety, the battle of Winchester. No part of the battle was fought upon the river; the heaviest fighting was within sight of the spires of Winchester.

Although bedell had no knowledge of it at the time, Getty's division of the Sixth Corps, to which the Vermont brigade was attached, with the First Division under the gallant Russell, on the 18th of September was again encamped for the night at Claremont, near the deserted house where he lay. In the early morning, before the army moved, General Russell had presented to Colonel Luke, the owner of Claremont, his favorite mare. She had been wounded, and her master left her, under Colonel Luke's promise that she should be cured and cared for. "A few hours afterward," said Colonel Luke to the writer, "her brave owner lay dead upon the field, but the descendants of his favorite mare have ever since been celebrated as the best-tempered and most admirable horses ever bred in the valley." Had the officers of the Vermont brigade known that Bedell was living and where he was, he would have had many friendly visitors.

The main body of the Union army struck the road from Berryville to Winchester, followed it about five miles, and crossed the river at the ford. They followed the road through a wooded ravine called Ash Run, the scene of much bloody bushwhacking, for about two miles, constantly expecting to meet the enemy. As they filed out of the ravine into the open country, on a hill to the northward of the road they saw Sheridan with his staff and knew that the battle was to be fought under his eye and command. With a cheer Getty's division formed its line of battle across the road, its left, held by the Vermonters, resting upon Abraham Creek, a stream running nearly parallel to the road to its mouth just south of the Opequan ford. Other divisions formed on their right, extending far north of the road, the Sixth Vermont being sent forward as skirmishers. The line being thus formed, the advance commenced.

The main body of the Confederate army was at

Stephenson's Depot, on the railroad about five miles north of Winchester. General Early and his staff were on a hill north of the Berryville road and within a mile of Winchester. As soon as he discovered the Union line, he sent aid after aid to hasten his army. In order to give the cavalry under Crook, Averill, and Merritt time to get into their desired position, the Sixth Corps was halted for two or three anxious hours and stood apparently waiting while Early's army was coming up. Ramseur and Gordon's divisions of the Confederate army arrived, crossed the road, and confronted the extreme left of the Union line. Fitzhugh Lee's artillery took its position in a wood north of the Berryville road.

The Union advance then commenced. It was over a rolling country in which there were some woods and very deep ravines. It is not our purpose to describe this advance. It is enough to say that it was not only against a fierce fire directly in front, but Lee's artillery from the wood north of the road enfiladed the Union line as it slowly moved forward. The slaughter was terrible, but nothing could arrest the steady forward movement of the Sixth Corps. They were fighting under the eye of Sheridan. They knew that they had not been held back, that they were not subjected to that murderous fire without a purpose. So they moved steadily forward down into the ravines, up their rocky sides, with ranks thinning at every step, until they had forced the enemy back to within a mile of Winchester.

There had been checks in this advance—once or twice the line had been broken and a part of it had been forced back. But it was re-formed and finally General Wright put all his reserves into the battle. The Sixth and the Nineteenth Corps now moved on, driving the enemy, capturing many prisoners, and finally overcoming everything in its front and clearing its part of the battle-field.

Now the result of Sheridan's combinations began to be apparent. Crook's cavalry, together with that of Averill and Merritt, had made a long *détour* to the northward and had finally got into position. Then it was that Sheridan rode along the whole line of battle of the Sixth Corps, in the midst of the storm of bullets, shouting as he passed each brigade, "Crook and Averill are on their left and rear, and by Heaven we've got them bagged!"

A member of General Early's staff who stood with the writer on a slight elevation just north of the Berryville road, almost thirty years afterward, gave the Confederate view of the closing moments of the battle. "From the top of this hill," he said, "General Early had given his orders during the day. From this hill aid after aid had been sent to hurry forward the troops from Stephenson's Depot, and yonder," pointing to an elevation on the east side of the road, "is where Gordon and Ramseur first formed their line. From yonder wood Fitz Lee enfiladed the Union lines with his artillery, inflicting heavy losses upon them. Farther east in another wood was a Federal battery. They fired upon us until they got our range, and their shells came so close that we had to retire to the west side of the hill. All through the long day our lines had stood firm and unbroken. We had begun to hope that they could not be broken by the Federal force. But suddenly over yonder hill, far beyond our left and in our rear, came a large body of cavalry. Before it our lines seemed to melt away and sink into the earth. It was a heart-sickening spectacle to us. The cavalry moved on at a slow gallop, but the disappearance of our line moved with greater speed. It was not checked until it reached Ramseur's division, on our extreme right. That division retired, without breaking, around the easterly side of Winchester into the pike beyond. The remainder of our army, broken and disorganized, fled through the streets of the old town, pursued and many of them captured by your cavalry. The pursuit was continued to Kernstown, three miles beyond. There, after sunset, Ramseur made a stand and gave his pursuers a volley. They inferred that we had been met by a reinforcement and the pursuit was over."

The result of the battle of Winchester and that

of Fisher's Hill, only two days later, turned the route of the Union army away from Berryville, and the Confederates being still farther south, this part of Clarke County was left to the rule of the strongest. Camp-followers, bounty-jumpers, and tramps of the lowest species swarmed over the region like an Egyptian plague. How that solitary woman managed to suppress the fact that a Union soldier was recovering from his wounds in her house must always remain a mystery. Except that it was very slow, there was nothing very unusual in Bedell's progress toward convalescence, but many days elapsed before he could move about the room with improvised crutches on his remaining leg. Seldom did a day pass when Mrs. Van Metre's house was not visited by one or more of the wandering vagabonds. Bedell was in her own room. She took good care to let every lawless visitor know that it was her room, and those who had any decency kept out of it. But if they insisted upon entering it, she was not at the end of her resources. There was a door into a dark room in the mill. Sometimes the patient was bundled into that room. Sometimes she boldly threw open the door and told them to enter and insult the privacy of an undefended woman if they would. They had never yet done so, for they were too cowardly to brave her indignation.

The patient did not suffer now for want of the

best nursing. Dick and Ginny his wife and Peter Dennis had faithful hearts under their black skins, and the attention of Dr. Osborne was unremitting. He was now supplied with strengthening food and proper medicines. The journey to Harper's Ferry was made once every week. The old horse improved in his strength and paces, and his appearance on the road had become so common that it ceased to attract the attention of those who lived along the turnpike.

But the cautious woman did not relax her vigilance. She knew that except those who were exempted from the draft by age, the men who remained at home were equally destitute of honor and humanity. It would be a congenial work for one of these miscreants to inform the criminals living in their mountain dens of her journey and of the time of her return with her supplies, and thus furnish them with an opportunity to rob a woman. Once only was she interfered with in this manner. It was not unusual for these wretches to lie in wait for the traveller. Ash Run and other ravines had become so notorious that no one passed them except under the protection of a guard. An accomplice in the town had informed one of these parties of her journeys to Harper's Ferry and her return with supplies. The fact that she was a woman, which would have secured her immunity from every decent thief, was only an additional inducement for these rascals, because they could rob a woman with less risk than a man. There were four of them who on one occasion lay in wait for her. It was in a wood through which the turnpike passed, nearly a mile from the nearest house. But they had not counted upon any resistance. Her escort was a factor neglected in their preparations. They had halted the old horse. They had dismounted, left their horses in the wood, and now two on each side of the wagon were endeavoring to persuade the driver to ransom her horse and wagon by a peaceful surrender of the contents of the latter. There was a sudden rushing sound like the coming of a furious storm; there was a gleam of steel in the moonlight—the sickening sound of cutting edges upon living flesh, and when the storm had swept past, the four thieves lay wounded upon the roadside. Their wounds were not mortal, but they were desperately painful and effectually disabled every one of the robbers. The old horse jogged onward to his destination, and the attack upon his driver was never renewed.

There was only one ground of suspicion, on the part of the agents of the Sanitary Commission at Harper's Ferry, of the good faith of Mrs. Van Metre's weekly requisition. It was the extraordinary quantity of whiskey required for the consumption of the invalid. Her explanation, however, was very satisfactory. There were a number of old men in the neighborhood not included in the drastic terms of the Confederate draft. It was impossible to conceal from these patriarchs the fact that a Confederate woman was nursing a wounded Union officer who was attended by the country doctor. But every one of them was amenable to the seductive influence of good whiskey, which some of them had not tasted since the beginning of the war. The promise of the weekly ration secured the silence of every one of these venerable gossips, and under the influence of such a beverage as they had not tasted since the peaceful ante-bellum days they were easily convinced that such a shattered wreck as the lieutenant could not greatly imperil the Confederacy. The use of old Bourbon for these diplomatic purposes was recognized as a political necessity; the secret was kept, and the draft of Mrs. Van Metre was good for anything contained in the Sanitary treasury.

The strength of the wounded officer soon returned to such an extent that he was able to dictate a letter, which his willing amanuensis committed to paper; and it was not the less precious to her who received it because of the illegible scrawl which stood for his name, the best he could make with his stump of a hand. It was duly directed and on one of Mrs. Van Metre's journeys posted. In due time she carried back to her patient a bulky letter in a beloved handwriting, postmarked among the Green Mountains. She opened it, handed its sheets successively to her patient, and listened while he read. The tender confidences between husband and wife under such circumstances are not for the eye of the public. The letter told of the health, comfort, and hope of his wife and children—his happiness was so supreme that for a moment his nurse forgot her own sorrow and her triumph was complete.

CHAPTER XIV.

THE BATTLE-FIELDS OF WINCHESTER—THE SEARCH FOR A FORGOTTEN GRAVE—AN ACT TO BE HONORED BY BRAVE SOLDIERS AND EMULATED BY TRUE WOMEN.

THE spires of the old town of Winchester have overlooked some tragic scenes. The visitor of to-day will find a quiet city of moderate size presenting no features of general interest, in which men buy and sell and get gain much the same as in other peaceful communities. But in one of its shaded suburbs there is a cemetery in which rest over five thousand Confederate dead. Many graves have neat white marble slabs upon which are inscribed the names and regiments of each silent tenant. And there is one very noble monument. On its base is recorded the fact that beneath it are buried over eight hundred and seventy unidentified soldiers of the Confederacy. This city of the dead is not neglected. It is inclosed within an artistic fence of iron, the gift of Charles Broadway Rouss, a former citizen of Winchester.

Adjoining it on the north side is the Union

cemetery with its more than five thousand dead. Here too is a noble monument to more than twenty-seven hundred unidentified Union soldiers. This greater number of the unknown is said to be due to the fact that the Union forces were strangers from the North, while many of the Confederates were residents of the valley.

These ten thousand lives were the harvest of death in the battle-fields of two campaigns in this immediate vicinity. How sad the story which these two monuments tell! Every one of these soldiers had a home—many of them wives and children, mourners for their dear ones, long awaited but never to return. Yet this abundant harvest of death was from small battle-fields compared with Antietam, Gettysburg, or the Wilderness, each of which was more fruitful in the casualties of war.

How many acts of heroism worthy of historical record were performed within sight of old Winchester! Here, just east of the turnpike which leads to Martinsburg, was the bloody battle of July 20th, 1863, when the Union forces coming from Stephenson met the Confederate army, and after a desperate fight forced it back through the city and then held both city and field. There was hard and weary work for the Federal surgeons, with their own and their enemy's wounded. When on that moonlit night the women of Winchester came out as volunteer nurses, they were glad to receive them and gave them enough to do. It was under yonder great oak that Miss Tillie Russell found the frightfully wounded boy, his chest deluged with his blood, his face pale, his body writhing in an agony of pain all the more intense from his constrained position. She raised his head from the ground into her lap and supported it by her arm. The movement gave instant relief to his pain and he fell asleep. But when she sought to change her position his agony returned. She called a surgeon and explained the situation. "His sleep may save his life," said the surgeon. "It is the only thing that will." She made no farther complaint. She was willing to suffer to save him. Through the long hours of the dreary night she sat motionless holding the boy's head in her arms. Her friends had returned to the town. She was alone among the dead—her arm was almost broken by the weight upon it. But there she sat while the boy slept all through the dreary hours of night until the morning. And his life was saved—he is to-day an honored citizen of the valley. The heroine deserves some better recognition than she has hitherto received.

Fourteen months later, from this hill General Early hurried up the divisions of Rodes and Gordon from Stephenson to meet the Union lines formed from Abraham's Creek across the Berry-ville road, and on yonder field they faced each other during that long September day. On our

Lieut. Bedell

left is the wood from which Fitzhugh Lee's artillery so long enfiladed the Union lines. Far on the right is Dinkle's barn in front of Ramseur's division, where the Union General David A. Russell led the charge and lost his life. Almost in our front is Hackwood, where an aid of General Early was delivering an order to another general, who fell dead while the order was being read. But there is neither time nor space here to describe the heroic deeds witnessed on this battle-field. It was dotted with Confederate and Union dead at the close of the battle, and the slain of both armies were buried where they fell.

"We fought Early from daylight until six or seven o'clock and drove him from Opequan Creek to and beyond Winchester." Such was the dispatch sent in the evening of September 19th by General Sheridan to General Stephenson at Harper's Ferry. With so much material the temptation is strong to describe the part of the Vermont brigade in this fierce conflict; but such an account does not fall naturally within our scope, which is only to give an idea of the area and extent of the field.

The battle of Winchester was followed by that of Fisher's Hill, on the 21st of September. A part of the Union army then passed nearly a month in traversing other sections of the valley. It went up the valley as far as Mount Crawford, a few miles beyond Staunton, and thence down the valley through Harrisonburg to the vicinity of Front Royal; then by a rapid march through Newtown and Middletown it rejoined Sheridan near Martinsburg, where the whole force remained until shortly before the 19th of October. During this time the army of General Early was kept south of the Union forces.

By following these movements on the map, it will be seen that for a month after the battle of Winchester there was no Union or Confederate force in the vicinity of Berryville, if the small body of irregular cavalry under Mosby is excepted. Mosby had, as he claimed by way of retaliation, executed Union soldiers, because he said that Custer had hung some of his men, claiming that they were not a part of the Confederate army. Mosby did not otherwise violate the laws of war.

This month was the harvest of the bushwhackers and bounty-jumpers in Clarke County. They came down from the mountains, where they carried on their single industry of illicit distillation, and robbed the dwellings of the living and the graves of the dead. No road was safe from them. Ash Run and other ravines were the scenes of daily assassination.

Notwithstanding these perils of the road, Mrs. Van Metre did not omit her weekly trips to Harper's Ferry. Upon one of them she learned that one of the Union officers who had protected her property and eaten at her table had fallen in the battle of Winchester. He had earned her gratitude by gentle and courteous treatment, and now when she heard that he lay in a nameless grave on the field where he had fallen, she instantly resolved that his resting-place should no longer be forgotten and unknown if she could find and place a stone over it. The search would be difficult; no one knew the pit or ditch where he lay, and there was even a discouraging rumor that his body had been robbed of his uniform and buried without any indication of his rank or name.

Except Dick Runner and Peter Dennis, whose color permitted them to be humane, she had no one to assist her in her care for her patient. She must therefore take up the search for the officer's grave alone or aided only by one of these colored men, while the other was left in charge of the house. She took Dick Runner into her confidence. The next day and for several subsequent days she left her home, with the old horse and rickety wagon, in the early morning, and did not return until evening. She was sad and weary, but not discouraged. What was she doing? The answer should be inscribed in letters of gold on a monument more lasting than granite. For this young Virginia matron, bearing the burden of her own sorrow, nursing a wounded man back to life, still found the time and energy to search all over that broad battle-field, day after day, for the grave of a comparative stranger. The search was long—many would have abandoned it. But Heaven would not permit such energy to fail of success. After many days she found the grave she sought. A board had been driven into the earth at its head on which she was just able to decipher the name of her casual acquaintance. But the inscription was almost obliterated. A few more storms and it would have been illegible, and the officer would have slept forever among the unknown dead.

What she saw would have repelled and turned away any man or woman whose heart was not brave and true. The thin covering of earth which had been hastily thrown over the uncoffined body had been washed away by the rains of autumn; the limbs and portions of the brave man's body were already exposed, for the dogs to gnaw, the carrion birds to peck at, and the foxes to mangle. Willingly did Dick Runner, in tender memory of "de young gen'l'man," guard his body through the night and until his watch was relieved next day. At her own cost, out of her slender purse she paid for a decent coffin, hired two laborers to disinter the remains, to place them in the coffin, remove them to Winchester, and there, with the silent prayer of at least one mourner, to inter them in the Union cemetery. She placed a suitable stone at their head for their permanent identification.

Such conduct cannot fail to receive the commendation of all right-minded men and good women. The account is imperfect unless the final result or Mrs. Van Metre's reward is given. I will state it in the words of Colonel Walker in his "Vermont Brigade in the Shenandoah Valley," published in 1869:

"Then she addressed a letter to his friends, giving them the information which she possessed, and they subsequently recovered the remains, thanking God and their unknown benefactor." It is to be fervently hoped that they did not fail to acknowledge and reward her heroic conduct as she deserved.

CHAPTER XV.

A SIDE VIEW OF THE BATTLE OF CEDAR CREEK, WITH "SHERIDAN TWENTY MILES AWAY."

The wounded lieutenant by the middle of October was on the high-road to recovery. The faithful service of the country doctor, supplies from Harper's Ferry, and careful nursing were doing their efficient work. The longest pair of crutches which the stores of the Sanitary Commission could furnish were ingeniously lengthened by Peter Dennis, and enabled Bedell to demonstrate that the loss of his leg had not deprived him of the power of locomotion. He was inclined to test it by more frequent exercise in the open air than was consistent with his personal safety. The tramp-thieves were more numerous than ever. They infested the region and had entered Mrs. Van Metre's house a dozen times a day. To exclude them would excite their suspicions and their cupidity, and they were too powerful to be resisted. They were given free access to every room in the house; nothing apparently was concealed from them, and they were finally satisfied to desist from despoiling a lonely woman who had nothing useful to them of which she might be robbed. How she evaded their vigilance and allayed their suspicions is simply inexplicable.

Bedell now began to suffer from another want. Almost six weeks had passed since he was wounded. He had no clothing except that which was on his person when he fell. His nurse had managed to provide him with some undergarments much too small for him, and Ginny had displayed great ingenuity in washing and changing them while he slept. But now that he wanted to dress himself and take more exercise in the open air, he felt intensely the want of a complete change of clothing which was not saturated with his blood. His natural habits of cleanliness intensified this desire, and made him almost reckless in his determination to have a new suit of undress uniform or its substitute.

Again with excellent judgment his preserver considered the situation, decided that he must have his change of clothing, and that the duty of providing it was cast upon herself. About twenty miles up the valley, where Cedar Creek winds around the base of "Three Top" and Masanutten Mountains, was the present camp of Sheridan's army. With it were supposed to be the baggage-wagons of the Vermont brigade. In the wagon of the Eleventh Vermont was the lieutenant's portmanteau, or, as it was commonly called, his "gripsack," which contained a complete change of clothing and many other articles of which he felt the want. He was now becoming strong, he was an adept in the art of concealing himself, and the three colored persons were perfectly trustworthy. There was no reason why she could not as safely leave him for a trip to Cedar Creek as for one of her weekly journeys to Harper's Ferry. The distance was no greater, and she could go and return with the "gripsack" in a single day.

By practice the lieutenant was able to write with his left hand a brief letter or order to the colonel or the quartermaster of his regiment for the delivery of his clothing to the bearer, and to sign it with his name. It was his first communication to his regiment since his fall, and the letter also explained the change in his handwriting and the reason of his absence. Provided with this authority, Mrs. Van Metre again provisioned her patient against her temporary absence; the old horse was harnessed to the old wagon, which seemed to grow stronger with use, and this time accompanied by Nannie Koontz, her young niece, the brave woman at early dawn started for the camp at Cedar Creek, not less than twenty miles away.

She reached the camp without misadventure. The officer of the picket took her directly to the headquarters of General Getty, who commanded the division of the Sixth Corps to which the Vermont brigade was attached. To him she delivered her letter and explained her errand. With the speed of the wind the rumor reached the regiment that a messenger had arrived from Bedell and that he was still living. Men and officers of the Eleventh hurried to headquarters and, when the rumor was confirmed, demanded to see the bearer of the welcome news. Without any hesitation she came out from the general's tent, and to the crowd that gathered around her modestly told her extraordinary story—how and where she found Bedell, his neglected condition, his danger, and his improvement. Then she explained her errand and invoked their assistance in procuring the clothing for which she had come. How she impressed the Vermonters may be gathered from the account written by their Colonel Walker at the time:

"Our feelings of wonder and admiration were most intense as we learned from her simple story that our favorite who was dead was alive again, and felt how much true heroism her modest words concealed. She had plainly totally abandoned herself for weeks to the care of a suffering enemy, and yet she did not seem to realize that she deserved any credit for so doing or that every woman would not have done as much." In short, she captured the affectionate interest of the whole Vermont brigade.

The afternoon was drawing on before they

would release her from the last of their inquiries. Then they had to give her the disappointing intelligence that the baggage-wagon of the Eleventh Vermont, of which she was in search, was still at Winchester. But they would not permit her to think of returning to her home that day.

They loaded her with the hearty attentions of the camp and made many preparations for her return journey. The old horse was well cared for; a tent was prepared with two beds for herself and niece to occupy, and everything was done to enable them to pass the night in comfort and security.

"Here again," she said to the writer long afterward, with the simplicity of a child, "it seemed as if the Lord directed me. The beds were tempting, we were both weary, but I would not permit my niece to remove her clothing nor did I remove any part of my own. Dressed as we were, we lay upon our cots and fell into a refreshing sleep. Just before dawn I was awakened by the incessant howling of a dog. I was dreadfully annoyed and wondered why some one did not put a stop to that disagreeable noise. I am sorry to say that I wished that dog was dead. But his howling continued, and as we could neither of us sleep we arose, performed our ablutions, put on our hats, and waited for daylight.

"Suddenly there was a shot—another—and then the irregular dropping fire which I knew

THE BATTLE OF CEDAR CREEK. 139

too well was that of a skirmish-line! Then the curtain of the tent was drawn away and a voice said, 'Dress and get ready as soon as you can!' At the same moment there was the crash of musket-firing only a short distance away. 'We are ready *now*,' I said. The side of the tent was drawn away and there stood our horse ready harnessed to our wagon. An officer helped us into it. He said to an orderly, 'Take this horse by the bit, go by a road' (which he described) 'as rapidly as you can. It will bring you into the Winchester pike. Follow it—stay with these ladies until you know that they are out of danger. These are General Getty's orders—there is an attack along our whole line! Now go!' Even as he spoke the sound of the shots almost drowned his voice and the shells from a battery of artillery began to form their curves over our heads."

Mrs. Van Metre had heard the opening guns of the battle of Cedar Creek, of the 19th of October. Defeated at Winchester, crushed again at Fisher's Hill, the indomitable veterans of Stonewall Jackson's corps had retreated up the valley, gathered in their stragglers, received some reinforcement, and now had turned upon and attacked their pursuers. Sheridan had been summoned to Washington for consultation, and on this morning of October 19th was at Winchester. Some criticism has been expended upon him for leaving his army subject to such an attack, especially as a signal to General Early had been taken from the Confederate station on Three Top Mountain, coming from Longstreet, saying, "Be ready to move as soon as my forces join you, and we will crush Sheridan." If such a signal was sent, Sheridan was right in disregarding it, for the writer is assured by Major More, of Early's staff, that none of Longstreet's force joined Early in the valley, and none of them were present in the battle of Cedar Creek. It may as well be conceded, for it is certainly true, that this battle was a remarkable instance of a defeated army recovering itself and with slight reinforcements turning upon and surprising its victorious enemy. No soldier would have anticipated such an attack, which would have been successful had not the plunder of the camp proved too tempting for the hungry men by whom it was captured.

Mrs. Van Metre had left behind her all the noise and confusion of a surprise.

> "And there was mounting in hot haste; the steed,
> The mustering squadron and the clattering car,
> Went pouring forward with impetuous speed,
> And swiftly forming in the ranks of war!"

The sounds of battle were not new to her. Without obstruction, by a circuitous route which took her outside all the camps, she reached the turnpike and was able to plan her future movements.

THE BATTLE OF CEDAR CREEK. 141

What was she to do? She was on the highroad to Winchester. From the sound of the firing over so broad an area in her rear, she inferred that the attack was made along the whole line of the Union army. If that army was defeated, the turnpike would be its line of retreat and would be crowded with fugitives. She was familiar with the dangers and terrors of a retreat. If she became involved in a herd of panic-stricken fugitives, army wagons, and ambulances, escape would be almost impossible. If the attack failed and Early's army was driven up the valley, the road would be crowded with reinforcements hurrying in his pursuit. She could leave the turnpike and by taking any one of the cross-roads on her right, get outside the crowd and reach her home. But then she would not accomplish the object of her journey. The clothing of her patient was in the baggage-wagon of his regiment at Winchester, to which the turnpike led. To Winchester she resolved to go, unless prevented by obstacles which she could not overcome.

The orderly sent to protect her promptly decided not to neglect the opportunity of escape afforded by her conveyance. He took the reins and the driver's seat and forced the old horse over the rough road at a speed which threatened at every step to wreck the old wagon. It was fortunate that he did so, for Ramseur, Gordon, and Pegram's division of the Confederate army had struck a division of Crook's corps and Kitching's division so heavily that they were swept away like leaves before a storm. The veterans of these divisions were for the moment a terror-stricken mob, that filled the turnpike, carried away the Eighth Vermont under brave Colonel Thomas, placed across the pike to arrest their flight, and apparently led the army in a mad race for Winchester.

As the morning drew on Mrs. Van Metre knew that the battle had become a defeat. Louder and louder swelled the roar of cannon, the rattle of musketry, and the din of the conflict behind her. Once or twice the pursuit seemed to be checked for a moment, then to be resumed with the rush of a furious storm. All over the southern horizon rose the black smoke of battle; now it seemed stationary—now to be coming nearer. Her new driver, in spite of her remonstrances, lashed the crippled horse into a mad gallop which could not long endure, in his effort to keep in advance of the oncoming crowd of fugitives. But it was useless: the pursuit was too vigorous. She was overtaken, surrounded, overwhelmed by horsemen, men on foot, yelling drivers of army wagons, from which escape now seemed impossible.

Here fortunately she was relieved of the driver. He had dashed the conveyance over obstructions which sorely tested its strength, and a repetition of such experience would wreck it. He now saw some better means of escape and promptly deserted the woman he was ordered to protect. She took up the reins, and by watching her opportunity turned out of the road and the crowd and made her way more slowly across the fields.

About ten o'clock, as she supposed, there was a change. The sounds of the battle no longer seemed to advance. The smoke cleared away, the rattle of musketry was less continuous, the stream of fugitives diminished, the crowd passed on and left the turnpike almost clear. Had the retreat stopped—the pursuit been checked? She determined to take all the chances. If it had, she might still reach Winchester and accomplish the object of her journey. The turnpike was unobstructed, and she turned into it again.

The moment when she came to this conclusion was synchronous with another event which deserves mention. The Sixth Corps, which at the first attack had formed in line of battle and, as other divisions had been overwhelmed, had fallen back about four miles, preserving its formation, had now reached the limits of its retreat. Wright, as brave a soldier as ever fought, was in command. He threw his corps square across the pike, and the Nineteenth Corps formed in its rear. It became a rock against which the waves of retreat dashed in vain. Early's whole army from a commanding eminence in front opened upon it with musketry and artillery. They pounded Ricketts' division for half an hour, and finding that they made no impression, turned to the more agreeable work of plundering the Union camps. Sheridan had good warrant for saying in his report in substance that the Sixth Corps was the "only infantry that confronted the enemy from the first attack in the morning until the battle was decided."

The crowd of fugitives had disappeared. The turnpike was clear. There was not a man, an army wagon, or a vehicle upon it. Suddenly coming over the next ascent appeared a moving body. In the advance was a horse, apparently without a rider. He was followed by a small number of mounted men. All were moving with great speed, but the horse in front seemed to be gaining on the others. They rushed along the pike with the speed of the wind. As they came nearer to her, she discovered that the foremost horse had a rider, but he lay so close along the shoulders and neck of the animal that he seemed a part of him. The head of the horse projected in a line with his neck, the rider clinging to it as if he would reduce the resistance of the air to the minimum. The uniform rise and fall of the bodies of horse and rider, as regular as a pendulum, the effort of both to forereach to the last possible inch with every bound, was the perfection of horsemanship, an ideal exhibition of muscular action. The rider was a short and rather a heavy man who knew that his horse was doing his best. For his heels, armed with sharp spurs, were turned outward, as if he scorned to touch his steed with their points, and his reins lay loose upon his horse's neck. The nostrils of the animal expanded with every respiration, and the white foam from them flecked his flanks or spotted the uniform of his rider. Never were horse and his master more thoroughly agreed. The stride was gigantic. The speed could not have been increased if the fate of a nation had depended upon it. Mrs. Van Metre turned her wagon aside from the travelled part of the road to allow the cavalcade to pass. With open mouth and powerful respiration, the steed showed that he was doing his best. His companions used every exertion to equal his pace. But he was rapidly gaining and opening the space between them. As they swept by the woman and her stationary vehicle and rapidly passed from her sight, she knew that the battle was on and that Sheridan was not many miles away!

The noble animal with his invaluable burden had not much farther to go. Only two miles farther to the south, a brigade of Custer's cavalry had now been thrown across the pike to intercept the advance of the enemy. Just in their rear General Getty's division of the Sixth Corps was posted across and at right angles to the turnpike.

It was a perfect dam to the current of fleeing men. On their right Taylor's battery opened upon their pursuers. With the check, confidence returned, and the fugitives again sought the position of their several commands. The Sixth Corps, Taylor's battery, and Torbert's cavalry were already in position—the tide of retreat had been turned when the black steed and his rider came into their view, attended with a mighty tempest of cheers. He swept along the line to the position of General Wright. He saw at a glance that the chief of the fighting Sixth had already turned the tide of defeat and the faces of his men in the opposite direction. "I am glad to see you here, general!" was the soldierly greeting of General Wright. "By Heaven! I am glad to be here!" was the emphatic reply of the man who was now to pluck victory from the very jaws of defeat.

The remainder of the battle of Cedar Creek was upon a field far in the rear of the emissary of the wounded officer. Her way to Winchester was now unobstructed. How many men would have been brave enough to follow it, with one of the great battles of the century raging in his rear, which might at any moment again overwhelm him in the desperate confusion of a retreat, when by a simple change of course he might in a short time be outside the danger-line? This woman thought only of her errand, which was to re-

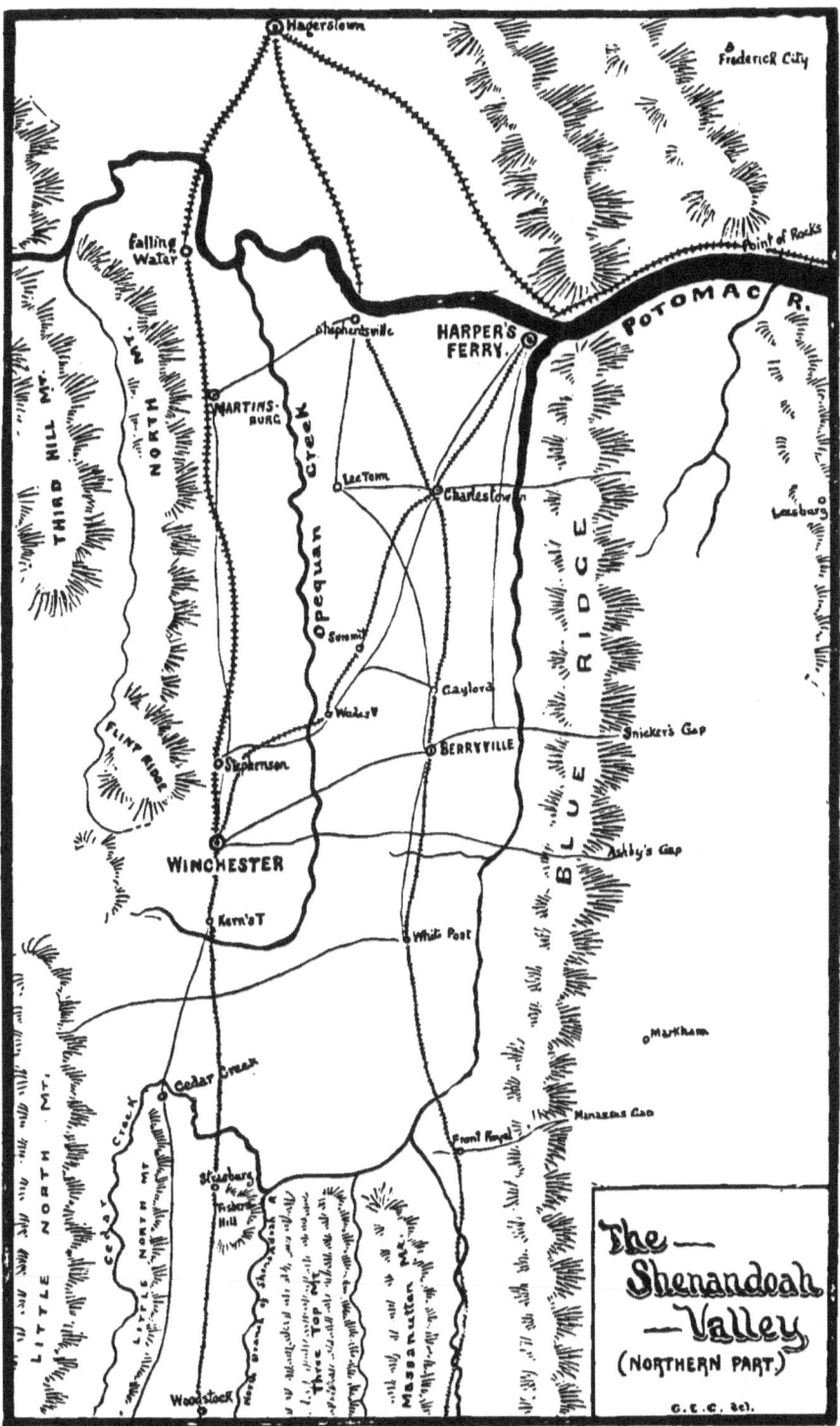

lieve the discomforts of her patient. If she turned to the right or left her mission failed. She therefore kept straight on, and without meeting with any farther actual obstruction, about one o'clock she reached Winchester.

In some way, never clearly explained to her, she found that her errand had been anticipated. Outside the town on the turnpike she was met by a soldier who wished to know whether she was not in search of the baggage of the Eleventh Vermont Regiment. She admitted the fact. "Then come with me," he said, and took her at once to the quartermaster of the Vermont brigade. Here her story was accepted without objection or question.

They would have kept her at Winchester over night, for the few Vermont boys whom she found there admired her simple, unostentatious energy. But in her quiet way she said that Bedell would be anxious about her—he would fear that she had been involved in the great battle which had been fought, and of which she did not then know the issue. She thought it would be better if the boys would assist her in getting the change of clothing for their brother-officer, and then let her go to him and relieve his anxiety.

To such good sense and excellent judgment the boys had no objection to make. They procured the "gripsack" of the lieutenant, containing his new uniform. Then they had a caucus, in which the agent of the Sanitary Commission took an active part. A committee of this caucus decided upon the probable necessities of Bedell under the circumstances. The package was made up (omitting nothing), and after a good feed for the old horse and an excellent lunch for the driver and her niece, the cavalcade was ready to start for Berryville. The conveyance was more liberally freighted than upon any previous occasion from Harper's Ferry. She had not only secured the desired change of clothing, but a liberal supply of the linen and underclothing which was so necessary to the comfort of the convalescing officer.

To the casual reader of history this exposure by a young and inexperienced woman to the actual dangers of battle may appear incredible. One would suppose that, terror-stricken by the actual peril to life, she would seek every opportunity to escape and to place herself outside its dangers. But it is one of the merciful compensations of war that it suppresses personal fear, and that those who are within the range of its terrible missiles accept the situation as a necessity.

I cannot better illustrate the fearlessness of this woman in accomplishing her object on the day when she knew a great battle was being fought, which might at any moment overwhelm her, than by an account of an incident which I myself saw, and for the accuracy of which I am willing to be held responsible.

THE BATTLE OF CEDAR CREEK. 151

When General Early attempted to capture Washington by a surprise in July, 1864, it was necessary to connect the forts by which it was defended by earthworks. Forts Stevens and Reno, on either side of the extension of Seventh Street, were connected by a ditch and corresponding earthworks. In their construction it became necessary to destroy several small dwellings and to remove their occupants with their household goods. One of these dwellings was occupied by a colored family, another by an immigrant from the Emerald Isle, both having large families of children. Their furniture was removed into the street or highway on the crest of the hill, just where it was supposed the attacking force would attempt to enter the city. The officer in command, aware that they would be under fire, urged the heads of these families to retire to a less exposed position under the hill, where he offered to carry their household goods. They would not consent. In the afternoon the attack was made. Shells were sent screaming over the place and the air was humming with the sound of minié-balls. Singularly enough the two families appeared to fraternize. The children were playing, the mothers attempting to cook their food by an open fire in the middle of the street, while the masters of the two households, extended on the ground, contentedly smoked their pipes as unconcerned as if the missiles of death which filled the air above them had been the notes of innocent singing-birds. Neither of these families could be induced to withdraw to a place of safety, because if they did they might become separated from and lose their little household furniture. There they remained while the fierce cannonading hurled its missiles above their heads, and I believe ultimately escaped all injury.

Some insensibility to danger of this kind must have protected this brave woman on that fearful day. From the early morning when she left the camp at Cedar Creek until nightfall when the cavalry of Custer had driven the attacking army up the valley toward Strasburg, there was not an hour—no, not a moment—when she was not within ear-shot of the roar and the dangers of a great battle which might at any moment overtake and overwhelm her. Yet she kept straight on, turning neither to the right nor the left, not for one moment losing sight of the object of her journey.

At Winchester she accomplished it, and in the early evening reached her home in Berryville, where she found her patient delighted with her success, which so much contributed to his comfort, but more disposed to render thanks to the Almighty for her protection and deliverance from the perils of the day.

CHAPTER XVI.

THE TERRIBLE HARVEST OF WAR—THE PREPARATION FOR THE ESCAPE OF THE WOUNDED OFFICER.

THE conduct of General Sheridan in destroying the military value of the region in his last campaign, and his burning of dwelling-houses in some instances, have been severely criticised and have presented an interesting subject of inquiry, some of the results of which will be here given.

General Sheridan was ordered to act under the instructions given by Lieutenant-General Grant to General Hunter on the 4th of August, 1864, by which he was directed to "take all provisions, forage, and stock wanted for the use of your command. Such as cannot be consumed, destroy. It is not desirable that dwellings should be destroyed, they should rather be protected, but the people should be informed that so long as an enemy can subsist among them, recurrences of these raids must be expected, and we are determined to stop them at all hazards."

When Sheridan left the valley for the last time, he reports that he "commenced moving back, stretching the cavalry across the valley, from the Blue Ridge to the eastern slope of the Alleghanies, with directions to burn all forage and drive off all the stock, etc., as they moved to the rear, fully coinciding in the views and instructions of the lieutenant-general, that the valley should be made a barren waste. The most positive orders were given, however, not to burn dwellings."

He declares that "the whole country from the Blue Ridge to the North Mountain has been made untenantable for a rebel army. I have destroyed over two thousand barns filled with wheat and hay and farming implements; over seventy mills filled with flour and wheat; have driven in front of the army over four thousand head of stock, and have killed and issued to the troops not less than three thousand sheep."

He sometimes exceeded his instructions as to burning dwellings, of which he gives the following instance: "Lieutenant John R. Meigs, my engineer officer, was murdered beyond Harrisonburg, near Dayton. For this atrocious act, all the houses within an area of five miles were burned. Since I came into the valley from Harper's Ferry, every train, every small party, and every straggler has been bushwhacked by the people, many of whom have protection papers from commanders who have been hitherto in the valley."

It would be extremely satisfactory if all the

murders in the valley could be fastened upon the vagabonds who recognized no lawful authority. But the evidence is conclusive that Mosby on one occasion ordered seven Union prisoners to be hung. One of them escaped by killing his guard, another got away in the darkness, and five were executed. Beyond this the evidence fails to affix the guilt of murder on any Confederate authority. That the old men who were exempts from the draft should be guilty of such crimes is extremely improbable. When the outlaws were so numerous that they infested every ravine and murdered every straggler, there was certainly no occasion for attributing such horrible crimes except to those who were always ready to commit them.

It was unquestionably true that every one who wore the Federal uniform, if separated from his regiment, carried his life in his hands. Colonel Toles, chief quartermaster of the Sixth Corps, and Captain Buchanan, commissary of the Second Division of that corps, were both murdered near Berryville, and such murders were too common to excite discussion.

Whoever may have been responsible for the existing lawlessness, the danger of the convalescent officer was constant and very serious. His wounds were slowly healing and his long confinement became irksome and finally intolerable. He knew that for him discovery was death, and yet his desire for exercise in the open air became so overpowering that he insisted upon it at any risk. The weekly trips to Harper's Ferry began to excite discussion, and the demands of the venerable topers for whiskey became so exorbitant that the Sanitary Commission threatened to repudiate them altogether.

As his improvement continued and he felt his former strength returning, Bedell experienced an attack of another disease to which the sons of the mountains are peculiarly susceptible. The doctor said its scientific name was nostalgia, but he preferred the good old-fashioned name of homesickness. In some cases it might be ridiculed as a disease of the imagination, but cases had occurred in the Vermont brigade where it had had a fatal termination. In Bedell's case the attack was severe. His longing for his home, his wife, and his family became irresistible. It deprived him of his sleep by night and of his comfort by day. There was only one cure for it. He must be sent home. If not assisted he would undertake the journey at any risk. Again his nurse determined to accomplish his cure and to make it as free as possible from danger.

As the lieutenant lay upon his bed or was bolstered up in an easy-chair in her room, which she had surrendered for his use, and when the whole household were devoted to his care, he began to reproach himself for his selfishness and to think that it was high time that he gave some thought to the troubles of his benefactress. He determined that in this respect his conduct should be promptly reformed. Now, as he watched her and appreciated the sorrowful, far-away look upon her face, he knew that one who was dear to her was constantly in her thoughts, and he suspected that her exertions in his own behalf might be inspired by the hope that they would in some way benefit her husband and promote his release. It was clear to him now that her active mind sought constant employment, for if it was occupied by her own anxieties she would sink under the burden. She had given some information about her husband when he told her of his dream, but it was very indefinite. Very gently now he made farther inquiries about him. Then he knew how true a woman his preserver was, for her emotions overcame her and she sought relief in giving way to them. He persisted in his inquiries. He drew from her that, although not a voluminous correspondent, her husband had not failed to write her a brief note every week since he entered the army. But since his reported capture in May she had had no news of him. Nothing, she feared, but death, or sickness that was very near to death, could account for his silence. Her anxieties had increased with time, and now when she gave her confidence to the man she had saved, she had to confess that she sorrowed almost as one without hope.

Her grateful patient attempted and did not wholly fail to comfort her. He referred to his singular dream, and while he again disclaimed all belief in dreams, he still maintained that it might be a Providential intimation that her husband was living—that he had been ill, but was now in good hands, which would account for his silence.

That same night as he lay upon her bed and thought of his own wife, his home, his sufferings, and all that this wife of his enemy had done for him, he registered in the depths of his soul a solemn resolution that when once again under the protection of the national flag, before he went to his own home, before he did anything for himself, he would find her husband and restore him to her arms. Nor did this resolution ever weaken, as we shall see in the sequel, until the desired result had been accomplished.

This point settled, he devoted himself to the problem of reaching Harper's Ferry. Both armies having been withdrawn, there was no longer any protection for property or life. The lawless element ranged over the country at will. The wretches who now came out of their dens in increased numbers have already been described. They belonged to neither army—they robbed Unionist and Confederate with equal impartiality —they were literally the enemies of the human race. Any one might shoot one of them with perfect confidence that he was doing justice to a murderer. Every man's nand was against them; cold-blooded murder was their commonest crime.

They were so numerous that scores of them ranged through Berryville daily. There was no day when some of them did not visit the house where the wounded officer was secreted, for by some means they had been informed that a Union soldier was somewhere about the premises. On one occasion they came upon Mrs. Van Metre unawares, and the lieutenant was saved only by her boldness. This time they insisted upon searching her room. "Search it!" she said, "if you are indecent enough to invade the privacy of a woman." And she threw the door wide open. They took a hasty look inside and went away. "I knew," she said, "that the lieutenant would conceal himself as well as he could when he heard my voice. He was standing behind the door with a revolver in his hand as it was thrown open."

For a man of his conspicuous size, with only one leg, to make his way in safety to Harper's Ferry was a problem very difficult of solution. While he was revolving it in his mind, one of the patriarchs whose secrecy had been secured in the manner already stated, came to him under the burden of a great sorrow. He had a favorite pair of mules which were very dear to his acquisitive soul. They had been in great peril every time the sharp-toothed rake of war, in Federal or Confederate hands, had harrowed the valley. But with great caution he had always managed to save them from capture until now. When Sheridan decided to leave the valley, he determined not to leave behind him an animal that could draw a load or feed a soldier. None so useful as a mule could escape the quest of his troopers. The old farmer's mules were discovered, dragged from the hiding-place which had so many times effectually secreted them, and their owner's heart was broken.

He had given up all hope of recovering them, and was trying to reconcile himself to their loss by the excessive absorption of sanitary stimulants, when through the mysterious communications of the colored people with each other the old farmer learned that his mules were in the corral at Martinsburg. Changes in the position of the Union army had made Martinsburg instead of Harper's Ferry its base of supplies, and all the animals brought in by the last Sheridan drag-net had been collected there. With many sorrowful expressions the old farmer bewailed the loss of his beloved animals. He repeated the story so many times that Bedell came to detest the very name of the species. He could not give the owner any relief nor could he prevent the constant repetition of the story. When finally it became obvious that the stricken mourner would pay any price within his means or do anything in his power to secure the return of his mules, the lieutenant began to consider whether he could not in some way make the situation available for his own escape. One day when the owner was bemoaning his loss for the hundredth time, Bedell ventured the cautious intimation that if he were safely delivered within the Union lines at Harper's Ferry, it was just possible that an exchange might be effected of his own crippled body for the coveted animals. No trout ever leaped for a fly, no son of Abraham ever pounced upon a shekel, with greater avidity than the mule-owner did upon the intimation. Bedell had no more authority to contract for the surrender of these animals than Satan had to trade off the earth from the top of a high mountain. But he decided to take the risk of making the contract and of procuring his authority afterward. The impatience of the other party was too great to be restrained by a matter so insignificant as want of authority. He insisted upon closing the bargain at once—upon commencing the work of preparation that night, and it was only with great difficulty that Bedell could induce him to postpone the arrangements for the time indispensable for careful precautions.

His first necessity was the co-operation of his hostess and preserver. As the shades of that evening were beginning to fall, while the active woman was moving about the room, putting everything in its place for the night, he said abruptly:

"I think I have a plan by which I can reach Harper's Ferry!"

The announcement disturbed her. When she spoke after some hesitation, her cheerful voice was obviously the result of a strong effort to control herself. "I ought to congratulate you," she replied, "and I am truly glad to hear what you say. You have been such a sufferer here, you must so long to see your wife and children, that I am almost as glad as you are that you are soon to be with them. But it will be lonely here when you are gone. You have given me so much to do and think about that I must say I shall miss you very much."

"Mrs. Van Metre," he said, "when I leave this place you will leave it with me. Only one thing could induce me to go without you. I would if I could leave you with your husband. That we cannot hope for now. I have been selfish, looking only to my own troubles, quite long enough. I wish now to prove that I am not altogether ungrateful. I will not leave you here, exposed to increasing dangers. I want you to say now that if I decide to attempt to reach Harper's Ferry you and your niece will go with me. From that place we will go and find your husband."

"I do not think I can say that. A true wife should never leave her husband's home without his consent. When he returns she should be there to welcome him."

"But he cannot return. He is a prisoner. Madam!" he said very earnestly, "in that dreary room from which you took me I have suffered fearfully. There have been many hours when I was near to death. At times I have feared that I was losing my mind. Once, as you know, I thought I had seen your husband. That was unreal, but I cannot resist the conviction that he lives, that he will only be found after a long and difficult search. But for you I should now be in my grave. Shall I now leave you when I can assist you in the search for your husband? I can find him. I know I can find him. I do not know that any one else can. No, I shall not leave you! And what nobler duty can there be for a true wife than to go with me to search for her husband?"

"Heaven forgive me!" she said plaintively, "for I scarcely know what to do. Your words are very convincing, yet I am not certain where my duty lies. I must think of matters which you will not consider. There have been those who are base enough to say that my care for you involves disloyalty to my husband and to the cause in which he has enlisted."

"Do not wound your true heart or sully the lustre of your noble deed by any reference to such wretches," he exclaimed. "You know that

I respect you as I do the memory of my mother. I know that your heart is as pure as a diamond. Enemies shall not come between us to destroy our ability to assist each other. You must let me decide for you!"

"I cannot, I dare not now! Give me until to-morrow morning to pray God for his direction."

CHAPTER XVII.

THE ESCAPE.

The plan of the escape matured before the final decision of Mrs. Van Metre, and was the combined invention of the officer, the old farmer, and Uncle Dick. Secrecy was now more important than before. The old recipients of the chief stimulant would not be provided with it when the patient had left and were rather interested in his detention. It had been difficult to restrain their gossip in the past. It would be more difficult if it involved his departure. The plan must be kept from their knowledge as completely as from that of the tramps who infested the valley.

Mysterious sounds during the night now became common in the stable of the Van Metre homestead. It was kept carefully locked under Uncle Dick's exclusive control. A second horse, a good match for the spavined Rosinante, came to keep him company. Wheels, whiffletrees, and other parts of a two-horse farm wagon and of a double harness were collected there. In the course of two or three days a substantial wagon was constructed, strong enough to carry a load to Harper's Ferry over roads, now in November, worse than ever. From different contributors a ton or more of hay, enough for the load, was secured. A crate over six feet long, in which crockery had been imported, was procured, openings were made on its four sides for ventilation and defence, and then Uncle Dick announced that the ship of the valley was ready to receive cargo.

The straw mattress was to be laid upon the bottom of the wagon with a Winchester rifle, revolver, and cartridges. On the mattress was to be placed the officer. The crate was then to be put over him, and with its contents firmly bound to the body of the wagon. The lieutenant could lie extended or sit up, and from the forward end and two side openings get a view of more than one-half the horizon. The openings from the crate were to be loosely covered by the hay and so concealed from observation. In the event of an attack, the obstructions to sight could be readily removed from the inside.

It was the cautious old colored man who had insisted upon these defensive preparations. In one of the mysterious ways known only to those of his own color, the particulars of which he would not disclose, he had become satisfied that an attack would be made by a party of not more than two or three persons, who were on the watch and who had kept the opportunity to themselves in order to secure larger shares in the booty. Bedell had tested his fidelity too thoroughly now to disregard his counsels.

The arguments of her patient finally prevailed, and with some misgivings Mrs. Van Metre decided that herself and niece would accompany Bedell and share the dangers of his attempt to reach Harper's Ferry. She had few preparations to make—they could take nothing with them—the slightest suspicion of their purpose would be fatal to its success. It was after midnight when the officer was laid upon the mattress with his fire-arms and crutches by his side. The crate was laid over him and its openings were carefully arranged. The whole load was firmly secured to the wagon, which was then piled up with its ton's weight of hay. A binder pole of hickory over the top, lashed to the axletrees at either end, held the load firmly in its place.

The old farmer had allowed the rumor to get abroad that on a certain day he intended to go with a load of hay by an unfrequented route to a place of contraband trade not far from Harper's Ferry, where, if he was favored by fortune, he would exchange his forage for a goodly quantity of that liquid comfort now so much prized by himself and his non-combatant neighbors. In this manner an interest in the success of his expedition was excited, so general that the veterans could not suppress their hopeful anticipations, and they came very near to wrecking the enterprise.

The preparations were perfected with all the skill of the united judgment of all the persons interested; the load made up; the unmatched horses harnessed and secured to it; and Uncle Dick by the aid of a ladder assisted his mistress and her niece to the seat arranged for them on the top and carefully laid an army blanket over them.

Then there was a touching separation between the mistress and her servant. "Dick!" she said as with her taper fingers she clasped his great horny hand, "you and Ginny have been devoted to me ever since our troubles began. It does not look now as if I should ever be able to repay you. If I cannot, I am certain that such fidelity as yours will be rewarded in heaven."

"Chile!" exclaimed the negro, "now don't you go on talking dat way, and make yo' old uncle feel bad jis when he wants all his pluck. Co'se we done for yo'—yo' was all the friend we had. But we's no time now to talk about dem tings. We know massa is in trouble Dere is jis one man who can find him an' help him. He is a good man. I hear him say in his sleep, he would give his other leg if he could bring Massa Van Metre back to yo'. Now de last words of ole Dick is, 'Yo' stick by de Union officer—yo' take his 'vice, and when yo' come back to Berryville yo' goin' to bring Massa Van Metre wid yo'.'"

"I believe you are right, Dick. I will follow your advice. Good-by! God bless you!"

The driver was now in his place just in front of his two passengers. The stable-door was opened; the team and its load emerged from the stable and turned into the road leading northward. The north star out of the depths of the blue sky shone in her face. Farther east beyond a peak of the Blue Ridge, a spike of crimson flame shot up toward the zenith. The solitary surviving tenant of her poultry-yard greeted her with a burst from his clarion. Tiny thrushes all along the wooded road seemed to invite her forward by their varied morning song. Her heart rose at the sound. All nature seemed to urge her forward and to say to her: "As nothing so graces the true American woman as mercy and relief for the suffering foe or friend, so nowhere is all that a true woman holds priceless safer than under the protection of the gentleman who wears the American uniform, whether it be blue or gray."

And now the farmer manages the reins with a full sense of his responsibility for the safety of his passengers and freight; the old horses seem inspired by a new energy, and all feel that every step in advance is a step toward safety. Over every rough piece of road the horses carefully pick their way; when the road is smooth they strike into a lively trot, and before mid-day nearly the whole route is covered and the spires of Harper's Ferry are just visible in the distance.

But their escape was not yet assured. Out of the nettle of a great danger they had still to pluck the flower safety. Within a half-hour of the end of their journey the road descended into a ravine nearly a mile in length, darkened by rocks and trees. In the darkest part of this defile, two horsemen suddenly descended upon them from among the rocks by the roadside and ordered the driver to halt. They were young men, not more than twenty-five; they wore no uniform, but a glance told the brave woman that they were of the worst class of camp-followers, as cold as any Indian to whom the torture and murder of his wounded captive is a pleasure.

And the old farmer knew their faces. Originally thugs from Baltimore, they had enlisted and deserted from both armies, and were under sentence of death by a court-martial for murdering the wounded at the first battle of Winchester. By the treachery of one of their guards, they had been able to murder two others and escape to the mountains. They were the men of whom Dick had been warned. They had kept close watch, and mounted on fleet horses had waited until the team had selected its road, and then by fast riding over another road had passed them and arranged this ambush.

"What fer do you want to stop me on the

highway?" asked the old farmer. "I am going to sell a load of truck, good for nothing to you, but might keep my folks from going hungry. Let me alone to go my way," he said, and with a cool eye to future proceedings he, as if by accident, swung his team partially across and in the line of the road.

"Not much!" said one of the brutes, who stood opposite the seat of Mrs. Van Metre, while the other caught the horses by the head and stopped them. "We know all about you," he continued. "We have watched you for a week. You've got a Union officer under that hay. Maybe he'll live, if he's got greenbacks enough about his clothes. You, madam, have got money and things worth money on your person. We want the money and the man. Will you give them up without a fuss?"

"Gentlemen," said the lady very gently, "you are Americans, I hope, and gentlemen. I am going after my husband, who is a prisoner. I have but a very little money. I am a helpless woman. Will you not let me pass, with the little that is left to us?"

She might as well have appealed to cannibals, pirates, or hungry tigers of the jungle. "Now dry up an' get off'n that load," said the wretch. "We don't care shucks for your husband or your lover under the hay. We want your money an' your trinkets. Give them to me before I strip 'em off!" And the wretch seized her by the arm and was about to tear her to the ground.

There was the crack of a revolver. The grasp of the brute relaxed; he staggered a few steps and fell upon his face. A brief pause, and the louder report of a rifle, and brute number two at the heads of the horses slowly settled upon the neck and shoulders of his own horse, shivered, and fell on the turf at the roadside. Well did the women and the driver know whence these shots came, and that the foresight of Uncle Dick had saved them from capture or a worse fate.

"Drive! drive to the town as fast as ever you can, before others come!" said the anxious woman. "Let us get to the town before we are overtaken."

"Oh, yes, missus, we'll get over to the Ferry all right before very long." said the unexcited driver. "But don't you scare. I know these fellers. They meant to do this job alone—they hain't got no friends, an' they won't do any more damage till somebody sews up the holes in their clothes. But them horses of theirs have got the U. S. brand. I think we'll take 'em along. Maybe the general at the Ferry would rather swap my mules for these horses than for the sick kunnel."

With this monologue he proceeded to attach the bridles of the two horses to the rear of his wagon, while Mrs. Van Metre was begging him to hasten. But he persisted that there was no farther danger, and succeeded in inspiring her with a little of his own confidence. He then examined the men. Both were shot through the chest. One begged for water. "Well, well! I thought so when I see you two sarpents come out of the bush: you ain't no Union men nor yet Confederates. You're just black-hearted thieves an' murderers. You're one of the fellers I seen after the battle of Winchester. I was coming from Winchester way; two boys, one blue, one gray, both hard hit, was helpin' each other off the field. You an' another chap like you was stealin' after them with a big knife in your hand. 'Look out for that black devil, boys!' I yelled. One of the boys pulled his gun and one of the murderers ran. It was you, you black devil. You ain't dead now. You can't kill them sarpents no more'n pole-cats," he observed as he rolled him out of the travelled part of the road.

The delay while these reflections were going on had been almost intolerable to the poor woman, and little less so to the officer in his confined quarters. But it was over at last, and the driver was content to resume his seat, deliberately take up the reins, and tell his horses to "git." Within a half-hour afterward the conveyance was hailed and stopped by the picket on the Union lines.

To the questions of the officer in command of the picket, who demanded to know where he was going and what were the contents of his load, the farmer declined to make any answer. If he would not give any account of himself, the officer said he would be compelled to take him before the general in command of the post.

This threat did not appear to alarm him. On the contrary he said: "Young feller! you look bright and smart. If I was in your place that is just what I'd do. We're onfortnit prisoners of war. Take us befo' your onmarciless general!"

The clumsy wagon with its load of hay, drawn by the unmatched, half-starved horses, and its trembling female passengers were taken, under the direction of the officer of the picket, to the Union headquarters. Very deliberately did the ancient Jehu descend from his perch, throw his reins over his horses' necks, call for a ladder, and with its help and much courtly grace assist his lady passengers to descend to the ground.

The officer of the day directed the horses to be unharnessed, taken to the stables and fed. This done, the driver called his attention to the other pair. "Don't you think Uncle Samwell has some claim onto these hosses?" he asked. The officer had no doubt of it, and wanted to know whence they came and how he got them. "I will tell you the whole story when you take me to your general. I ain't a-goin' to make two bites of one cherry. You better take care of them hosses," he continued. "The fellers what had them won't come for them in a hurry."

"I will," said the officer, "and now come with me to General Stevenson."

"But I haven't got unloaded yet," he protested. "I 'spicions there's some other goods in that load you might like to see. Maybe some of you fellers will help unload the hay. Maybe there's suthin under it, I dun know!"

The hint of the old farmer fell upon listening ears. Stalwart arms, some with pitchforks, others with unaided hands, made short work of unloading the wagon. When the hay was removed there remained exposed the crate, covering the mattress upon which lay extended an officer in uniform, with his rifle, revolver, and crutches by his side. He was somewhat exhausted by his long ride and deprivation of air. They tore away the crate and aided him to rise. Willing hands handed him his crutches and raised him to an upright position upon his remaining leg. They brushed the dust and straw from his clothing, and scores of kind soldiers tendered him their good offices. He was almost destitute of strength, his face was very pale, the perspiration stood in great beads upon his forehead. Rough men turned away their faces in silence as they witnessed his heroic effects to control his emotions.

What a flood of thoughts must have crowded

his memory at that moment! The thunder and crash of battle, his fall, his amputations, his pains and weakness, his friends forced to leave him, his abandonment to death by the faithless ones who had promised to nurse him, his bitter loneliness when he was watching for death; the coming of his preserver, her bravery and her devotion, his long sojourn in the country of his enemies, with never an hour that was not one of anxiety and peril! It was all over now. He stood upon loyal ground, surrounded by his fellow-soldiers, with no barrier but distance, and that so easily overcome, between himself, his family and his home. Even his faithful nurse was with him. Was it strange that he was silent —that he was so overwhelmed as to be nearly unconscious of his other surroundings?

Almost in a whisper he asked for water. It was given to him; he raised his hand to his brow, and his face brightened as some thought came to him. Then his eyes anxiously wandered around the broad plaza, as if something was absent which he longed to see. They rested upon the foot of the tall staff at the top of which he knew the Stars and Stripes were grandly floating upon the autumn air. A look of profoundest gratitude covered his pallid face as he removed his cap, raised his eyes to it, and reverently saluted the flag of his country. The effort was too great for his weak condition. He trembled and would have fallen had not strong arms borne him to a chair.

Save for his whispered request for water he had not yet spoken. The crowd around him, which every moment increased in numbers, was as silent as himself. Brave men who would not have minded the thunder of cannon were so impressed by the pathetic interest of the situation and sympathy for the sufferer that they seemed to fear the sound of their own voices. After a few more minutes he appeared to summon all his faculties, turned to the officer of the day, saluted him, and said: "Colonel, I have a report to make to the general in command of this post!"

"I was about to offer to conduct you to him," said the officer. "I am certain that he will be as much pleased as we are to welcome your return among us. Would you like to have your companions see the general with you?"

"Certainly!" said the lieutenant. "They constitute very material portions of my report."

That was a memorable procession which the officer of the day now conducted to the quarters of the veteran General Stevenson, then in command at Harper's Ferry.

Arm in arm with the officer went the lieutenant, his once vigorous body emaciated, his face pale, his eyes sunken, his strength almost exhausted, his step uncertain as he strove to walk upon his single leg by the assistance of his unaccustomed crutches. He was followed by the woman who had been so heroic and energetic in the presence of real danger, but who was now so timid that she wished she could shrink into absolute obscurity, concealed from the sight of men. Her hand held that of her little niece, who was trembling like a frightened fawn as she looked to her aunt for protection. Next came the grizzled farmer. But his assurance had all left him, and now when for the first time he realized that he was actually in the power of his enemies, he appeared not to be quite certain whether he would not be ordered to be shot without trial or preparation. Officers and privates from the Vermont brigade and many other regiments followed, all anxious to testify their welcome back to life of the comrade long supposed to have been in his grave. They moved as slowly as a funeral cortége—they were admitted without any delay, and filled the quarters of the general in command to the overflow.

"General Stevenson," said the officer of the day, "it is my duty and my privilege to present to you a brave soldier, Lieutenant Bedell, of the Eleventh Regiment Vermont Volunteers! Lieutenant, I beg to make you acquainted with General Stevenson, in command of this post."

The veteran general would have taken his hand without a shadow of formality. The lieutenant retired a single step, saluted, and said:

"General, I have to report that I have been for some weeks absent from my regiment and within the enemy's lines, because disabled by wounds and unable to endure transportation. I have been concealed, nursed, saved from death, by the wife of a Confederate soldier, a brave and noble woman, whom I have induced to come with me to secure the release of her husband, a prisoner of war in our hands. I have been brought into our lines, secreted under a load of forage, by this farmer, who agreed to deliver me in safety at this post, in exchange for a pair of his mules appropriated to the use of the United States by order of General Sheridan, now supposed to be in Martinsburg. He has faithfully performed his part of the contract. I know I had no authority to make a contract to bind the Government, and yet if not inconsistent with the regulations I respectfully ask that the farmer may have his mules!"

"I confirm your contract!" said the general with great cordiality. "He may select the best pair of mules in the corral and take them home with him."

This arrangement did not satisfy the veteran agriculturist. He hesitated to interpose his objection. Standing with his battered hat in one hand, with the other he swept the few bristly hairs that stood upright on the top of his head, in imitation of the lieutenant's salute, and uttered his protest.

"General," he said, "it was *my* mules that I was to git. I wouldn't swap my mules for no two pair of the best mules in the valley. I raised them mules; I broke 'em. They're brothers, one ten, the other 'leven year old. They're wonted to every inch of my farm. Them's the mules I want; they're up to Martinsburg. Missus Van Metre's nigger seen 'em thar."

"If that is the case, you shall have your own mules," said the general. "I will see that the matter is looked into soon. Just now other affairs are of more pressing importance."

The mule-owner was preparing an elaborate statement of his objections to this arrangement, when the general turned him over to his quartermaster, with directions to see that he was well cared for, to hear his story, and if it was reasonable to give him satisfaction. One of his aids was directed to provide a room and all necessary accommodations for Lieutenant Bedell at the general's quarters. Mrs. Van Metre and her niece, he said, would be taken in charge by the ladies of his own family. As soon as Bedell was rested and refreshed, he wished to hear the particulars of his story.

CHAPTER XVIII.

REST AND PREPARATION FOR THE SEARCH.

GENERAL STEVENSON had with him the ladies of his family, who were then occupying a private residence in the town. The tide of war had rolled far up the valley, and they were living almost in the quiet surroundings of peace. To their care he committed Mrs. Van Metre and her niece. Our heroine was greatly changed. Now that the demands upon her energy were withdrawn, she became a retiring, sensitive young woman, unwilling to accept favors which she could never hope to return, yet determined not to seem insensible to the kindness of her new friends. They were equally cautious not to wound her pride or to force their favors upon her. With great caution, and largely by feminine instinct, they ascertained and, almost unknown to her, supplied the deficiencies in her wardrobe and that of her niece, and furnished her apartment with all those articles so necessary to the comfort of woman. She thought she ought not to avail herself of them; but she had so long suffered from their lack, they were so tempting, that she yielded, although she could make no present payment except by her thanks. These conveniences wrought a complete change in her appearance. She was now a refined, cultivated lady, very modest in her bearing, dignified in her carriage, and attractive in her whole appearance. But even the cheering looks and words of her new friends could not banish from her face that infinite sadness, that far-away look of anxious waiting for something or some one whom she feared might never come.

Nor was the crippled officer less fortunate in his experiences. Long accustomed to compliance with all the demands of a healthy regimen, his chief source of discomfort had been his deprivation of the luxury of the bath. He was now taken in hand by the valet of the general and the barber of the post. They were much more skilful, though they could not have been more willing or kind-hearted than Uncle Dick. When, after a liberal use of warm water, with his head properly tonsured, and what the new darky called a "fust-class shampoo," he left their hands, he was renewed in the outer man almost beyond recognition. Supplied by the general's orders with the missing articles of his uniform, he was once more and in fact Lieutenant Bedell, of the Vermont brigade, the pride of the fighting Sixth Corps, in all but the loss of his limb, to which he was now gradually becoming accustomed.

Then when, farther strengthened by a good

dinner, he was in a physical condition to do the subject justice, the big-hearted Stevenson demanded that he should give an account of himself during the long time when his brother-officers supposed he was in the other world. Many others were impatient to hear it, and he consented to relate it to as many of the boys as the room provided by the general would contain.

As a chronicler of events in which he had been conspicuous, the officer was not a success. Of those which concerned others he spoke eloquently—so eloquently that he excited the indignation of his auditors or touched their sympathies at his will. Commencing at the time when his friends unwillingly left him, with his supplies, in the promised care of the soldier and the wretches who had been paid to nurse him, he admitted that he sent away the nurse before he was robbed and deserted by the Asburys. He described how they took his supplies, promising to prepare and return with his meal; how long and hopefully he waited; how the conviction gradually became absolute that he was now abandoned by all; how the wind and rain whirled through the crevices during that long and dreadful night and the next long and dreadful day; then he knew he was growing colder, weaker, and his pain was increasing. He thought of his distant home, of those he would never see again. Would they ever know when and how he died? How long would he retain consciousness? Would any one find and bury him, or recognize him when he was dead? Was it wrong to wish to die soon— to have an end of his pain and grief in the sleep of death?

And now a thought came into his mind which led him to fight with a fierce determination. He would furnish the means of his own identification. They should not bury him with the unknown. At least his body should be returned after the war to the little churchyard under the Green Mountains!

In a pocket on his right side there was a pencil. If he could reach that! He would not sleep again, for he might die in his sleep; he could keep awake, and as soon as it was light enough in the morning, with his left hand he would print his name upon the whitest thing within reach! Now summoning all his strength, he tried to reach the pencil. Alas! he could not. He tried again and again, and each time he was weaker than before! Then he described his sickening sensation of failure: he must give up, he could do nothing. He began to long for unconsciousness and death. He brought the ghastly picture so vividly before their eyes that the hearts of his auditors were shocked and they hoped he would hasten to the end, and yet there was an attraction about it that led them to cry out when he proposed to omit an incident of the story.

"Comrades!" he exclaimed, "before my Maker I declare that at the very moment when I was giving up, when I knew my strength was sinking and I believed I was actually dying, I thought an angel burst into that dreadful room. I suppose she carried a lamp of some kind. It seemed like a great wave of sunlight, bringing warmth and hope into that place of darkness and desolation! I was glad; how glad God alone knows, and yet my mortification was intense. The colored man could do but little to make that room a fit place for any woman. I tried to tell her so, for I knew and I recognized her noble face. Then she silenced me as if I had been a child. 'Don't you speak, sir! not a word!' she said. The light showed a beautiful face looking down into mine, and a gentle hand and a soft handkerchief dipped in cold water were moving over my parched lips and clammy face. I tell you, friends, the drop of cold water from the hand of Lazarus would not have been so delicious to the fevered tongue of the rich man in torment as the touch of that moist hand was to me."

Then he told them how he was nursed into strength and then moved to Mrs. Van Metre's house; of the faithful services and discretion of Uncle Dick, his wife, and Peter Dennis. In short, he told them all that we have attempted to set before the reader. He omitted as much as his auditors would permit of that which concerned only himself—he was a helpless hulk, incapable of action, only to be acted upon. But when he spoke of his preserver, language was too weak for the expression of his gratitude and admiration. "Think of her, comrades!" he passionately exclaimed; "she is only a girl, even now. But did you ever hear of such courage, charity, energy, of such unselfish generosity? such untiring devotion of a woman to her wounded, helpless, suffering enemy? It was of little importance to mankind that she saved my crippled life, but her example ought to be preserved as a model for true women to imitate as long as there are wars among nations or virtues among men!"

"As he went on with the story," said one of his hearers, "officers and privates packed themselves in a circle around him. Every one leaned and crowded forward, with his hand to his ear, as if he feared to lose one word of the thrilling narration. It was a late hour at night when it ceased, not because our interest flagged or he had reached its conclusion, but because it was evident that he could not continue it except at the cost of physical exhaustion. The general with a very gentle voice said: 'We will hear the rest another time.' A brave, true chaplain raised his voice and exclaimed: 'And in the mean time let us all thank God for this woman—this noble woman, who enables us to say, this our brother was dead and is alive again—was lost, and is found!'"

PREPARATION FOR THE SEARCH. 187

That night, for the first time since he was wounded, the lieutenant slept without watchfulness or anxiety. He had much to do, and he wished to set about it without delay. He intended to take the early morning train for Washington, where he proposed to consult influential Vermonters and arrange for the release of the husband of his preserver. But when he awoke the sun was streaming into his windows, and the train for Washington had been on its way long enough to have already arrived at the capital.

A servant who had watched for his awakening brought him his breakfast, which he took in bed, luxuriously. He was then informed that the general wished to see him before he made any plans for the future.

General Stevenson received him with much cordiality. "Your system needs toning up, lieutenant," he said when he met him. "I have an excellent prescription for you. Be seated and take it at once." And he handed him a thick letter, only three days old, which bore a postmark in the Green Mountain State.

It proved to be just such a letter as a sensible, affectionate Vermont wife might have been expected to write under similar circumstances. It informed him of the health and comfort of his family, of their undying love, of their anxiety and sorrow when they heard of his wounds and his being left behind when the army retired, of their joy and that of all their neighbors when they learned from his last letter of his almost certain recovery through the nursing of a good woman. Would he carry to that dear woman the gratitude and love of his own wife? The writer had only one apprehension now. Her husband was still in danger in the enemy's country. She wanted him home!

"We have had a bad fright, dear," continued the letter. "But it is happily over now, and I can write you all about it. After we had read over your last letter so many times that we could repeat it from memory, Henry brought me his school atlas, and wanted me to show him where you were and the ways I would take to go to you. I took great pains to show him, for I like to know that the children are thinking about you. For two or three days the little fellow was very sober. Two or three times he said to me that you must be very lonely, and as you could walk only by the help of crutches, you must need some one all the time to get things for you. One morning very early I found that he had disappeared. I hunted for him, and as I did not find him I aroused the neighbors to assist me in the search. When I returned to the house I discovered that the map we had been looking over was torn out of Henry's atlas. It then flashed over me that the little fellow had started to go to you! At my request, our neighbor N—— harnessed his horse and drove immediately to the railroad station, which he reached before the arrival of the train for the South. There he found Henry half-concealed in a dark corner of the station. He asked him where he was going. 'I am going to bring my father home, sir,'' he said. 'It is a long way, and he is lame and cannot get away alone.' 'But,' said our neighbor, 'it is a long and expensive journey to your father, and you have no money.' 'I have some money in my bank,' he said; 'I will give all that, and when I tell them that I am going after my father who was wounded, fighting for his country, and has had his leg cut off and is lame, and we want him home, and there was no one to go after him but me, and I will work and get the money, I think everybody will help me! Don't you? Anyway, I must try!' He consented to come home, and he did not shed a tear until his arms were about my neck and his head lay on my shoulder. Then —but I think I will not tell how he grieved. So you see, dear Henry, that you need not mind the loss of your leg. Very soon you will have all the assistance you want from your own son.''

"General, I must go home at once. I cannot wait," said the officer as he finished reading the letter.

"That may be best," said the general. "But I have some information to give you, and before giving it I would like to know all the facts. Is there anything unpleasant in that letter?"

"No, I cannot say that there is. Would you like to read it?" he asked as he extended his hand.

"I think I would," responded the general. He took the sheets, and while reading them slowly turned his back toward the officer. There was a spasmodic twitching of his gray mustache. Once he removed and polished his spectacles after first wiping his eyes. Then he cleared his throat and faced the lieutenant again.

"It is not singular that you should feel drawn to your home, lieutenant," he said. "You ought to be proud of your son! Yes, and of his mother. If he lives and I live, and the country remembers the services of a battered old soldier, that boy shall go to West Point. He gets his sand from both father and mother, I see. It's the mothers, though, that make the boys. God knows what reason I have to say that!" he said with deep reverence.

"But I have tidings for you not quite so agreeable," he continued. "Mrs. Van Metre is ill—delirious. My family and the doctor don't quite understand it yet, but it seems that she has suffered so much that kindness overwhelms her. We fear she will have brain fever. It will be a sad, sad case if she does. I thought you should know her condition at once. She shall have the best of care, for I solemnly believe, Bedell, that she is the noblest woman I ever saw."

"General, you alarm me!" said the officer, "but you have settled one matter. I had thought I would go home for a few days, then return here and go with her to find her husband. But I should be a cur to leave her now. Heaven forgive me for thinking of it."

"You are a trump, my boy!" said the general, laying his hand upon Bedell's shoulder with a force that made his single leg quiver. "No man was ever the loser by doing the square thing by a woman, and certainly not by such a woman as she who saved your life. Now, if that brain of yours, which has been considerably stirred up recently, is settled so that you know, tell us what we can do for you. Mrs. Van Metre is in the hands of good nurses, who, for some reason which I do not know, say that it would not be wise for you to see her now."

"I know of one thing that I want now," said Bedell. "This stump of a hand of mine cannot yet do much with a pen. I want some one who will write a dispatch for me and afterward a letter."

The general touched a bell. "Bring me some telegraph blanks," he said to the messenger who answered his call. In a moment they were before him. "I will write the dispatch," he continued. "I know there is a woman who wants it. Here

I have the direction already written. What do you wish to say?"

"What is the charge for ten words?" asked the officer.

"Charge for ten words!" roared the general. "Man, are you crazy? Here you are, just brought back from the edge of the grave, and you want to count the words in which you shall tell the mother of your boy that you are safe under the old flag! No! no! tell me what you want to say. Give me the idea. I will write the message for you, for on my word I don't think you are capable of writing it—nor that I should be if I were in your place," he said after some hesitation.

Bedell complied. He would like to inform his wife, he said, that he had escaped from the enemy's country and was safe within the Union lines; that except for the loss of his leg he was almost well; that he would come home very soon, but there were some matters he must first attend to which would not detain him many days.

The general thereupon wrote the following after showing the direction:

"Your husband is now sitting in my quarters here, strong and well but for the loss of his leg and a part of his right hand. He was brought in by a brave and noble woman, who unquestionably saved his life, kept him concealed for six weeks, and brought him safely here. She, poor woman, is in deep trouble, for her husband is a prisoner in our hands, and she has not heard from him since his capture last May. Her exertions have overpowered her, and she has been stricken with fever. Your husband says he would be a cur if he should leave her in her present sickness and sorrow. I am no judge if the woman who wrote him the letter he has just shown me is not of the same opinion. Take the advice of an old soldier! Be patient! Stand by the brave woman who has so nobly stood by your husband, and, with the blessing of Almighty God, you and she shall both soon see your husbands."

The general signed his own name to the dispatch and marked it with the letters D. H. Bedell said it was admirable, just what he wanted, but the charges would ruin him.

"Do you see those capitals—D. H.?" asked the general. "They mean Deadhead! No charge. Free passage! If the telegraph company will not deadhead such a dispatch to such a woman as your wife, I have got no use for it and it will get out of my department double-quick!" He rang the bell. "Send this!" he said to the messenger who came. Then turning to the officer he said, "I will commission one of my aids to write your letter."

But Bedell declared that the dispatch conveyed

all that at present he desired to say to his wife. At all events, he would not write until he had more definitely determined when he would go home. First of all he wished to see Mrs. Van Metre.

CHAPTER XIX.

A TIME OF NEW TROUBLE AND ANXIETY.

IN his first interview with them, the officer saw that the faces of the surgeons wore a very serious expression. The condition of Mrs. Van Metre, they said, was very critical. Her danger was increased by their inability to account for her disease, upon which their prescriptions produced no effect whatever. Her temperature was very high, her pulse rapid, her delirium constant. She seemed to be tortured by her conscience. Her self-reproaches were pitiable. She said she was a bad, wicked woman. She had nursed, possibly saved the life of a Northern invader—of the enemy of the South. It was wrong—her countrywomen would all think it was wrong. Her prayers, her appeals for mercy were touching. She thought she was doing right; she had done it for her own husband! Should not a true wife do all she could for her husband? She had done wrong—she saw it all now. She did not ask pardon for herself, she was willing to die, but she implored the Lord to save her husband! She would not see Bedell, she could not hear his name;

she was a wicked woman because she did not let him die!

The doctors secured from Bedell a faithful account of all she had done, of all he knew about her. Her soul, he said, was as pure as an angel's. He had never heard but one intimation made against her conduct; that was by one of the robbers who attacked them on their way into camp; he had paid for his slander with his life. It was finally decided that in her grief for her husband she had sought occupation for her mind in the care of the wounded officer. That now he was out of danger, her grief had returned with greater intensity, and under it in her weakened vitality her mind had given way.

While this diagnosis was reasonably accurate, it did not give effect to their prescriptions nor lead her into the path of recovery.

Just then, however, something occurred which but for her delirium would have been more effective than any medical prescription. General Stevenson had been so impressed with her devoted conduct as described by the lieutenant that he had communicated the substance of it by telegraph, as soon as it came to his knowledge, to Secretary Edwin M. Stanton. That officer forthwith ordered the immediate discharge of Mrs. Van Metre's husband as a prisoner of war, and directed that well-known and knightly old veteran General Ethan Allen Hitchcock to write to her

A TIME OF NEW TROUBLE AND ANXIETY.

the letter which appears in our introduction to this volume informing her of her husband's release. This letter ought to have relieved all her apprehensions. But the assault of the disease upon the throne of her reason had been very severe. With all the obstinacy of delirium she refused to believe the good news, and even charged her nurses with kindly intent to deceive her. She persisted in her conviction that she had committed a crime for which there was no pardon. Even the excellent clergyman who, hearing of her troubles, came to reason and to pray with her, could make no impression upon her. Her temperature continued to rise, her fever began to develop more dangerous symptoms, and the skilled physicians who had her in charge said that unless it could be arrested, it would consume her remaining vitality and the end would come.

Poor Bedell was well-nigh frantic. From the very heights of happiness and hope he was plunged into the lowest depths of despair. He became almost as unreasonable as his benefactress in her delirium. He charged himself with her disease and her destruction. Nor could he for a time himself bear up against the sea of troubles which now appeared to roll its resistless waves over him. His long journey under the load of forage, deprived of a supply of air, had weakened him; his consciousness that her devotion to him was the proximate cause of his preserver's present condition so wrought upon his mind that he was ready to take to his bed, indifferent whether he ever rose from it again. Although the influences which wrought upon his mind were not unlike those with which Mrs. Van Metre was contending, the administration of remedies by the doctors produced some effect. They gave him powerful sedatives, and he ultimately fell into a broken, half-delirious sleep.

The railway station at Harper's Ferry was in such close proximity to the quarters of General Stevenson that from his room Bedell knew of the arrival and departure of every passenger train. He was even able to distinguish those to or from Northern and Southern routes of travel. One morning, after a restless night in which for the hundredth time he had reviewed the whole history of his acquaintance with Mrs. Van Metre, and was unable to draw from it any justification for the past or hope for the future, he fell into a half-waking slumber. The curtains were drawn to exclude the light from his windows; faithful colored nurses had been provided, who were directed to permit no one to enter his room except in their presence, for the breaking out of a new suppuration from his amputation was imminent. Should that occur, his condition might again become as desperate as it was when he was found in his deserted room.

On this afterward well-remembered morning,

as he lay dreaming of his home and of many things which gave comfort to his heart, he heard long before daylight the noise of the conveyances and other preparations for the early morning trains. Then there was the noise and bustle of their arrival, the clamorous solicitations of the cab-drivers for the passengers, the sound of wheels as the vehicles rolled away. Then all was still and dark again, for it was in the early days of winter.

He supposed that he fell asleep again and was dreaming of those who were so dear to him in his distant home. He imagined that he was in some new and deep trouble. Some one had come between himself and his wife and children and was intent upon keeping them separated. Weak and crippled by his wounds, he was powerless to resist. In the confusion of his dream he fancied he heard voices. One was that of his new colored nurse: "I ask your pardon, missus, but my orders was de strictest kind. De cappen mus' not be waked. No one mus' go into his room!" Then he fancied he heard another voice, strangely dear to him, entreating, "But I am his wife. I have the right to see him. Tell him that it is his wife that wants to see him."

"I cannot do it, missus," said the nurse. "I should be dismissed if I disobey de surgeon's orders, and if de cappen should die I would be shot. You mus' wait till daylight and see de doctor."

Then another dear, familiar voice seemed to say: "He is my papa! I want to see my papa! I will see him! No one shall keep me and my mother from my own dear father! Is this the door to his room? Stand aside, I say, and let us pass!"

"'Fore de Lord, I was afeard of dat little boy," the nurse afterward said. "Seemed like as if he was in command ob de post, and we had to get out ob de way. He march straight to de door, and say to de lady, 'Come!' Well! I did de bes' I could, but it was no use!"

Now indeed the door did open, and with an effect which reminded him of the night when his preserver first came to him in his desolation at Berryville. Some one ran across the room with a quick, light step and grasped his neck and spoke. He heard the voice of a boy exclaiming, "Papa! my own papa!" Then there was a slower, softer step, and in the dim twilight he saw approaching him the form which was dearest on earth to him. It was his own dear wife—it was no vision, no dream, all was real. He was awake, the arms of his wife and his boy were around him, their voices were in his ears, and, thank God, he was once more with his loved ones.

The advent upon the scene of a clear-headed, sensible woman promptly changed the appearance of things. At once, that very morning, before she attempted to give her husband any account of his home or of herself, she set about making herself the mistress of the situation. Her husband was only too ready to tell the whole story of Mrs. Van Metre and to sound the praises of the noble woman who had saved his life. His enthusiastic admiration might have excited the jealousy of some wives, but in this case it only filled her heart with love. She had long and repeated interviews with the doctors, who assured her that she must on no account see their patient, for the excitement would probably increase her fever and produce a fatal result. The old clergyman related his interviews with her, and finally the guests of General Stevenson took her into their confidence. From these ladies she secured much valuable advice and information. In fact, the conclusion arrived at was rather the result of their joint judgment than the opinion of any one of them. With the instincts of good and true women, they decided that Mrs. Van Metre was an intensely conscientious, faithful, and most devoted wife; that when she had long endured in silence her grief for the captivity of her husband and her anxiety for his safety, and when her nerves were irritated by the incessant sounds and perils of war, she had heard of this wounded, deserted, and dying officer. She had followed the impulses of her emotional nature, and with an undefined idea that some Northern woman might do for her imprisoned husband what she could do for his wounded adversary, she had devoted herself to the work of saving Bedell's life. The work gave her occupation—prevented her own grief from gnawing at and tearing her heart. She had succeeded. Now, when her patient was safe among his own people, when her constant devotion was no longer necessary, her own sorrow, her love for her husband, her doubts whether she had done right, her fears, had simply overwhelmed her like a flood. All the barriers of her firmness had given way, and the recent events in her life, that unselfish devotion which to others appeared so beautiful, seemed to her inexcusably selfish and base.

If this diagnosis of the situation was correct, Mrs. Bedell knew that it was the heart of her husband's preserver that wanted treatment, instead of her body, and that she could not be benefited by medical prescriptions. She was an energetic person, this woman of the Green Mountains, and her act swiftly followed her conclusions. As soon as she had decided upon her course, she went straight to the doctors and insisted upon her right to nurse the patient. They hesitated, argued; she was a stranger, they said. An interview with her they feared would increase the fever and excitement of the patient and might prove fatal to her life. Then they had no evidence of her skill and experience—in short, if she had been an ordinary woman they would have refused to permit her to see the patient, who, as they were constrained to admit, was rapidly growing worse.

She swept away their objections with a wave of her hand. "She will die, you say, unless there is a favorable change," she said; "your treatment has produced no good results. Why not, then, try mine? I think it is my duty to see and to nurse her. I would much prefer to see her with your consent. I have a better right to see her than you have to keep us separated. If I cannot obtain your consent, I must dispense with it!"

The doctors, who ardently desired to save the life of their patient, decided not to oppose her vigorous proceedings farther, and consented that she might see Mrs. Van Metre for five minutes only. She accepted the compromise with a mental reservation that she would do as she liked about complying with the condition as to time.

It was evening when she entered the sick-room. Very soft was her step as she approached the bedside and very slow the movement of her strong, cool hand as it stole around that of the patient, now hot with fever. She seated herself upon the bed; with her handkerchief saturated with some perfumed stimulant she bathed the dry, hot forehead and face; then her head drooped and she kissed the fevered hand which lay upon the coverlet. Then her arm quietly crept around the restless form and drew it toward her until each could feel the beating of the other's heart. Her face was very near to that of the weary patient now. Their lips closed in a long kiss, and the first words which fell in a whisper upon the ears of the sick woman were: "You have brought *my* husband back to me from the borders of the grave; we will go together and find *yours*."

There was no need that the new nurse should tell her that she was Bedell's wife—no need to thank her for what she offered to do—no need of any words between them. Their hearts were close together, speaking a language which both understood. Then for the first time since her illness the fountain of the sick wife's tears was opened. The tears of her gratitude mingled with those of her sister's affection on the same pillow.

The doctor who was on the watch, alarmed by the length of the stay of the new, self-appointed nurse, and really anxious for its consequences, now gently opened the door to call her away. By the dim light he could distinguish the forms of the two persons, but they were so close together that they seemed but one. The sick woman lay nearest to him; he saw the movement of her respiration, not short and feverish as it had been, but gentle and almost as slow as that of the strong woman in whose embrace she lay. As he came nearer he was still more surprised to find that the patient was sleeping, but the eyes of her new friend were wide open. He made a motion of his hand as if to invite her to rise and leave the room. With her hand which was at liberty she pointed to the woman sleeping in the clasp of her other arm, and as he declared afterward, she also gave him a glance of almost contemptuous refusal. "They have no use for me," he thought, and discreetly left the room.

An hour passed and then another—still the patient slept. They called Mrs. Bedell to her supper—she would not change her position. It was late in the evening when the patient awoke. There was a look of profound gratitude in her eyes, a healthy perspiration upon her forehead, and although she was not yet strong enough to be clothed, she was beyond question in her right mind.

The joyful news of the miraculous change in one patient was carried to the other and wrought an improvement in his condition almost equally extraordinary. His anxiety and loss of sleep on Mrs. Van Metre's account had so exhausted him that, as soon as it was removed, wearied nature reasserted her demands. Even his curiosity to hear why his wife and boy had come to him and of their adventures on their journey temporarily lost its influence. Just as soon as it was made clear to him that Mrs. Van Metre's fever had been arrested and that with proper care she would recover, his eyelids grew heavy and he was sound asleep before his wife had finished her story.

"Gentle sleep, nature's soft nurse, weighed the eyelids down and steeped the senses in forgetfulness" of both the patients who had been so long and so sorely tried.

There is an end even to the sleep of the laboring man—tired nature's sweet restorer—even to that which the Lord giveth to his beloved. When Mrs. Van Metre again awoke, it was to find her niece had been well cared for, and relieved of that anxiety, she yielded herself to the direction of her new friend with the docility of a weary child. Mrs. Bedell contented her with the promise that she would come back to her as soon as she had given her husband some account of his home and her journey. For this relation her husband was now impatient. She told it to him substantially as follows:

"Do you ask me why I came to you, Henry?" she said. "You should have known that your telegram would have called me to you from the borders of the grave. The story went through our town that you were not dead—that you had written me a letter while you were lying desperately wounded in the enemy's country—then that you had reached Harper's Ferry in safety, and from that place had sent me a telegram. The neighbors gathered at our house, heard and discussed your last dispatch. They could not understand why, if you were well enough to travel, you did not come home. I said that I could read many things between the lines of your telegram. I knew that the woman mentioned in it had done you some great service—I did not care to know what it was; that you considered yourself under a great obligation to her; that you would not leave her while she was ill and in great anxiety on account of her husband—for one reason because you would know that I wanted you to stay with her until she was well or had received some news of him. I was satisfied, but they were not. They said there must be something that kept you which you could not or would not tell me. You were either much worse in health than your general telegraphed or you were under arrest! Anyway they advised me to go to you at once. I said I had no money. They offered me four times as much as I needed. You may imagine that I did not require much urging to set out on a journey that would bring me to you.

"Next day I received a railroad pass from our good governor over the railroad to New York and back. Then the neighbors almost quarrelled over the children. There were four or five who wanted them until I returned. I supposed our boy would go to the father of his inseparable companion whom you know. He had said nothing, but he had been thinking. When he spoke, he said something like this: 'If my mamma goes, I am going with her to my father. He wants to see me just as much as he does her, and a man can do him more good than a woman. Then my mother wants me. I am not willing that she should start on this long journey alone when I can go with her and take care of her. You needn't try to stop me, for I have made up my mind to go.'

"I suppose the neighbors were rather amused by it, but I felt proud of the little fellow's manliness. Then some one said that as he was under ten years he would go for half-fare, and the conductors might pass him free if they knew our errand. So I consented that he should go. We started next day. I cannot begin to tell you how great an assistance he has been to me. He has made friends with every conductor—he has assured them that he was taking his mother to his father, who had his leg shot off in the war. No one asked him for his fare; he was manly but not forward with every one, and but for him I should not have got access to you when we arrived. I cannot help saying that I am very proud of him. This is the whole of my story, except to say that since you left us every one has been kind to us; and now, thank Heaven! you and I are together once more, and I hope never again to be parted."

Then her husband told his story and gave her a full account of the heroic conduct of Mrs. Van Metre. They were both of one mind. It was their first duty to protect her until they had found her husband and restored him to her loving arms.

A TIME OF NEW TROUBLE AND ANXIETY.

When the physician from the Green Mountains again returned to her patient from the valley, it was to find her fever abated and the light of a new joy in her eyes. "I have had such a lovely dream," she said. "I dreamed that an order had been issued for my husband's release by the Secretary of War. I hope it is one of those dreams which will prove true."

Mrs. Bedell had the very great joy of assuring her that it was no dream, but a fact which during her fever she would not believe. "Your husband's discharge is ordered," she said. "Nor is that the best part of the news. The conduct of his wife is commended by the Secretary of War as an example for the imitation of the good women of the world."

CHAPTER XX.

THE AFFLICTIONS OF THE MULE-OWNER—PREPARATIONS FOR THE SEARCH FOR A PRISONER OF WAR—THE SEPARATION OF THE FRIENDS.

THE proprietor of the mules had waited patiently until the sick were convalescent, and he now insisted that the contract with him should be carried out by the delivery of his animals. The quartermaster rather mischievously insisted that he did not see why one mule was not just as good as another, and that if the farmer was permitted to select a pair from the stock at Harper's Ferry he ought to be satisfied. But that arrangement no amount of bourbon fluid would induce him to accept. He undertook to satisfy the quartermaster that he ought to have his own animals. His argument promised to be entertaining, and was delivered in the presence of a large and amused audience. Inspired by a draught of stimulating fluid, he began:

"I s'pose them mules ov mine is pretty much spiled by this time," he sighed; "no mules could stan' what they've had to go through. I reckon."

"There is no possible ground for your fears,"

said the quartermaster. "The mules from Martinsburg have not been harnessed since the army moved. They have been well fed and ought to be in better condition than when they were captured."

"It's their morrils I'm afeard on. It's an awful resk. Look what company them mules has had to keep. They're soshiated with them ornary army mules. An army mule will spile anything not made of cast-iron. I was once got into a heap ov trouble by an army mule. They're the dangerousest, deceavinest hoss-kind that ever was foaled. They're artful enuff to cheat old Nick himself."

"I should think so if they were too sharp for a valley farmer. But tell me how they cheated you."

"It was this way. I foun' one ov them mules a-draggin' ov his halter — a-strayin' onto the pike. I picked up the halter. Why, he was the innocentest lookin' creetur—no butter wouldn't melt into his mouth. I went up an' patted him on the back. He kind ov sidled up to me like he wanted to be friendly—I scratched him an' he sidled up some more. His head was a-droopin'— his long ears slowly floppin' up an' down. His eyes was mostly shet, but I ort to have known that a look outen one corner ov his eye meant deviltry. But I didn't. The rest ov him was so lamb-like that I never thot ov his eye. I said to myself, 'This poor mule has got lost—he ort to be took care of or he'll starve. I'll lead him home and give him a feed.' So I started to lead him to my stable. But he braced out his four feet an' wouldn't go—jest stood still an' shook his head as if he meant, 'No go.' Still he seemed 'fectionate. He kep' movin' round an' kinder sidlin' up to me. I was pattin' him back of his hips an' a-sayin' to myself, 'They ain't many men as knows how to manage a mule—most men would whale this mule with a black-jack; that would hurt his feelin's an' make him contr'y; the way to manage a mule is to treat him softly —to reason with him. Now a mule is a good deal like a man—see how easy I can manage this one. I coax an' pat him an' he rubs up agin' me jest like a pet dog or a kit——'

"Jest then I was struck by suthin'—I thot it was the butt-end of a telegraph-pole. Suthin' dropped — it was me. The very stuffin' was knocked outen me. When I kem to myself I was a-layin' on my back in the middle of the pike. Abuv an' round me was a thick cloud of dust, an' in it, buzzin' an' whizzin' an' cris-crossin' every way, was about ten thousand mules' hind legs an' hoofs. It looked scary. I crawled right out ov that cloud, an' there as I lay on the ground, that cussed mule winked at me! Yes, sir, he winked at me! His latter end was cavortin' an' kickin' up all that cloud of dust an' mules' feet, an' the other end was wavin' his ears an' munchin' a Canada thistle!

"Jest then along come a nigger. 'Sampson,' I said, 'tie up that ar mule to a tree—cut a hickory gad an' whale him tell he squeals!'

"'Scuse me,' said that nigger, 'that is Uncle Sam's mule. I wouldn't dar hit him wid a stick. Don't you see de brand U. S.—Uncle Sam?' An' then up kem a teamster. 'Here, you cussed mule!' he said. 'What do you mean by running away? Who you consortin' with?' An' I'll be d—d if that cussed mule didn't trot up to that teamster an' lay his head over the man's shoulder an' laff—yes, sir, he fairly snorted! 'Yes, yes! I see,' said the man. 'Was they tryin' to steal you, Bob? and did you have a little fun with 'em?' An' then he laffed some more. An' I made up my mind to have nothin' more to do with no army mules. I want my own mules that I raised—that's got some morril principle. Sooner than take a pa'r of army mules, I'd change the wounded officer for three fingers of whiskey."

"You shall have your own mules, characters warranted, and the whiskey besides," said the quartermaster. "You deserve them for your story, as well as for bringing in our officer. But you must be patient until I can arrange for their delivery."

Although the order of Secretary Stanton implied that there would be no difficulty in finding

Van Metre, it was the strong conviction of Bedell that the search for him would be long and weary. He was decided not to leave his benefactress until he knew that the search was successful. There were many arrangements for him to make while awaiting her recovery. This was progressing favorably under the influence of the nurse from the Green Mountains. The latter's good sense and care gave her popularity among the officers at Harper's Ferry. She was a modest, simple, warm-hearted, but an intensely thorough woman. She was naturally reserved—her activity only appeared when the necessity arose. Then her reserve force was immense, and she seldom undertook anything which she did not accomplish. It is needless to say that she was esteemed and honored by all who knew her, and by those of her own sex beloved.

The universal favorite of the officers of the post was the Green Mountain boy of ten years, son of the wounded officer and his efficient wife. The youngster assumed all the duties and responsibilities of manhood. The attentions of others were pleasant to him, he said, but really he could not afford them much time. He had none for mere pleasure or curiosity. He must look after his mother; she wanted his close attention now that she had taken charge of Mrs. Van Metre. He could not leave his father to the carelessness of servants now that his son was on the ground.

The little time he could save from his father and mother should be devoted, he said, to military studies and practical work to qualify him to take his father's place in the regiment, for he would never be able to take the field again. He accepted, however, an honorary appointment to the Sixth Corps and his father's regiment, and when, decorated with the Greek cross and the cap and dress uniform of the corps, he was seen moving about the camp in the discharge of his duties, no one could fail to see that he was a born soldier. General Stevenson would have given him the title of brevet colonel, but he would not consent to outrank his father. He was known throughout the camp as the little colonel. He was a credit to the regiment as well as to himself.

One matter which Bedell felt bound to arrange was the contract about the mules. Those which the old farmer identified at Martinsburg were found to bear the brand of the United States. Instead of surrendering them, the officer in charge threatened to arrest the claimant. He, meanwhile, was faring so well in the camp and enjoying such an abundant supply of his favorite fluids that he was in no haste to bring his case to an issue. But Bedell brought the matter to the attention of General Stevenson, who cut the knot of the difficulty in a soldierly fashion. He ordered all the mules from Martinsburg to Harper's Ferry. When they arrived the farmer selected his beloved animals, and the general gave him a certificate that he held them by virtue of an exchange for a Federal officer whom he had delivered within the Union lines. He went away happy, and carried with him several valuable presents for Dick and his wife Ginny and for Peter Dennis. These were delighted to know that they were not forgotten by their mistress nor the wounded officer.

Then it was necessary to consult the paymaster. To his credit it should be recorded that he interposed no obstacles. He assisted Bedell to prepare his accounts, and the liberal supply of new and crisp greenbacks which he paid him was quite adequate to the wants of the entire party.

But when the lieutenant's application for leave of absence, founded upon his crippled condition, in order that he might accompany Mrs. Van Metre in the search for her husband, was presented to Secretary Stanton, instead of being granted it was marked suspended, and Bedell was ordered to report himself to the Secretary of War in Washington, and as soon as she was able to travel to bring Mrs. Van Metre with him. This check was very discouraging. It was inexplicable, inasmuch as the facts upon which the leave of absence was asked were certified by the surgeon of the regiment and by General Stevenson. But Bedell was a soldier, and notwithstanding the reputation of the terrible Secretary for inhumanity and a total want of human sympathy, he resolved promptly to comply with the order of his superior officer.

Under the constant watchfulness of her nurse and physician the improvement of Mrs. Van Metre was rapid. Her gentle ways, her cheerful submission to the directions of her energetic friend, won the hearts of all the ladies of the post, who were delighted in spite of her protests to make provision for all her wants which their sharp eyes could discover. A consultation with her was indispensable before the future course of the friends could be determined. Bedell wanted to hasten it, but his wife would not permit it to take place until she knew that all danger of a relapse had passed.

A bright, crisp November morning came, when a suitable carriage was found and one of our heroines took the other for a drive into the country.

The driver improved the occasion to impress upon the mind of her companion the fact that she was still physically weak and that she must submit without resistance to whatever plans for conducting the search for her husband should be adopted in the council of her friends.

"It would be idle for me to undertake any opposition to you," said the gentle convalescent, "for I am conscious that I could not succeed. From that first night when you came to me you have been able to control me at your will. I do not regret it, for you have won my entire confidence."

"I am glad to hear you say so," replied Mrs. Bedell, "for I want something from you."

"What is it, pray? What have I in my poverty which could be useful to you?"

"I want your niece—I want to take her home with me to the mountains. My husband seems to have come to believe in dreams. He thinks he has had a kind of revelation about your husband. He anticipates great difficulty in finding him. But he declares nevertheless that he will find him and bring him to our home in Vermont. Your niece cannot help you in the search. I will take her with me and love her as though she were my daughter, and when you come to us I will give her back to you."

"Perhaps your plan may prove to be the wisest," replied Mrs. Van Metre. "I am not shedding tears of sorrow. They come unbidden when I think what a friend you are in my loneliness. I will consider your request. I know I shall do what you ask in the end."

The ride seemed to give strength to the patient, and it knit these two souls together in the bonds of an enduring friendship. There was a council in which Mrs. Van Metre took her full share. It was decided that the little colonel should take charge of his mother and the Virginia girl of his own age, and escort them to the home under the shadow of the Green Mountains. The lieutenant and Mrs. Van Metre would proceed to Washington, take up the search for her husband, and never discontinue it until they found him. Then the three would go to Vermont, where all, reunited, would remain until this cruel war was over. They would separate now as soon as the arrangements could be perfected.

Mrs. Bedell now decided that Mrs. Van Metre was sufficiently strong to begin her quest. She could not be expected to restrain her impatience against farther delay. Her niece had become attached to Mrs. Bedell and was a great favorite with the little colonel. A re-examination of the cordial letter of General Hitchcock convinced them that they had not so much to fear from the terrible Secretary, and they were ready to leave Harper's Ferry.

Neither of them could leave a place where they had received so much kindness without regret. When on a bright winter's morning they found at the station the veteran Stevenson, many of the officers of the post, with the ladies of their families, and a multitude of private soldiers, assembled to bid them farewell, they knew the regret of the parting was not confined to the casual visitors. All the officers who had heard the story of what this woman of the valley had done for one of their comrades were there to tender her their respectful admiration, to bid her God-speed; other wives to thank her for the noble example she had set before the women of the country. All knew that her own life had been saved by the active skill of the woman from the Green Mountains, and energy is admired by the soldier almost as highly as courage.

The lieutenant was looked upon as one raised from the dead, and the little colonel was the favorite of all.

The latter was full of business; but he did not lose his head for a moment. Coolness was a special quality of Sedgwick's old Sixth Corps, and in the presence of these veterans he had the reputation of the Vermont brigade to sustain, and he did it well. He declined all assistance. His father had been provided with transportation. He had procured seats, and when the veteran general with moistened eyes and trembling voice had bidden Mrs. Van Metre farewell with the courtesy of a brave officer, he had only to escort her to her place. Lieutenant Bedell followed. The little colonel shook him by the hand, and as the train moved slowly out of the station he swung his cap and called for three cheers for Mrs. Van Metre. His call was responded to with a will which made the station ring from its base to the highest turret above its roof. Nor was the response less emphatic when some soldier proposed cheers for the departing officer.

The boy's work was nearly done. There was a proud look in the mother's eye and an amused expression on her face as she took his proffered arm and was led into the car, to the seat next the one in which he had already placed the young Virginian guest. Then when General Stevenson cordially took her hand and declared that he would make the future of her son his special care, and the boy took leave with the grace of a gentleman of every one who had come to see the party take their departure, it is not strange that her bosom swelled with some natural pride. The boy stood upon the rear platform of the last car and swung his cap as the train moved out of the station, and the salute of cheers which followed him was loud enough to drown the ringing of bells and the shrieking of steam-whistles. The train which moved northward bore a happy, grateful, affectionate, and proud wife and mother —grateful for the preservation of her husband, happy in his return, affectionate toward his preserver, and proud of her son. That which moved southward carried a brave and honorable soldier and a noble and true wife, who now was comforted by the reflection that she had done her duty, but whose heart was sad and sorrowful because her future still seemed dark and inscrutable.

And so they separated, followed by the kindly wishes of many friends, two of them to search after the person indispensable to the happiness of both families, the others to go to Vermont and wait for the reunion. There in due season they safely arrived—and there for the present our story leaves them.

CHAPTER XXI.

IN THE DEN OF THE OGRE, THE TERRIBLE SECRETARY.

UPON their arrival in Washington, Bedell went to a well-known friend of Vermonters who held a position in the civil service of the Government, and asked him to go with them when they called upon the much-dreaded Secretary. The friend, who had the advantage of a personal acquaintance with the chief of the War Department, declined the invitation. He knew something of the officer's story, and he also knew that the characters in it would need no other introduction. He assured the lieutenant that he might lay aside all his anxiety, as he would probably find the Secretary one of the most agreeable gentlemen he had ever encountered.

His friend could not remove Bedell's apprehensions. When the time came for them to go to the War Department, he afterward declared that he showed the white feather for the first and only time in his military career. He would have preferred to lead a charge against a battery of artillery, but when he reflected that he was performing his duty and obeying an order, his judgment reasserted itself and to some extent suppressed his fear.

On their way to the War Office, much to their surprise, they found themselves attracting general attention. They were the observed of all observers. Those whom they met upon the broad sidewalk turned to allow them to pass and then followed them with their eyes. They were quite unconscious of their unusual appearance. The lieutenant, six feet and three or four inches in height, in his new uniform, which fitted his gigantic figure, now filled out almost to its normal proportions; his head erect, his eyes full of energy and fire, with one-fourth of his body carried away, compelled to assist his remaining leg with the awkward wooden supports under his shoulders—by his side the small, girlish figure of the woman of the valley, very trim in her neat, dark travelling suit provided by her many friends at Harper's Ferry, her face concealed under the folds of a half-mourning veil, which she could not be persuaded that she should not wear—together made a picture which was impressive even in a city not unaccustomed to striking and remarkable exhibitions.

One of their experiences was long remembered. There was a French vessel of war at that time in the Potomac River, and a considerable party of her sailors were that day enjoying their leave on shore. They were in excellent spirits, rollicking along the avenue, here pausing to look at a public building, again inspecting and discussing in their lively foreign tongue anything peculiar which attracted their notice. Their eyes fell upon the singular pair coming toward them, one of whom they promptly assumed was a recently wounded officer. There was a sharp word of command in their foreign speech. It did not seem an instant when they were formed in two lines facing each other on the opposite borders of the footway. Then there was another order. Each man removed his cap, held it in his hand, and bowed his head. And there they stood, not boldly gazing into the faces of the pedestrians, but with eyes directed to the ground, until the wounded officer and his companion had passed between them and were some distance on their way. Then the Frenchmen broke ranks and resumed their promenade. It was a simple act, but it was noble in its simplicity. It was the natural, involuntary tribute of gentlemen wearing the uniform of common sailors to bravery and virtue. Had they know the history of the pair, their tribute could not have been more effective or more touching.

And so they made their way to the reception-room of the Secretary of War; that room which saw so many hopes dashed to destruction, so many scenes of sorrow and despair. After the summer of 1862 there were few mornings when it was not crowded. There were men and women there of all kinds and descriptions. There were speculators, dishonest contractors, thieves, knaves, bankrupt in money and character, and alas! so many with sad faces and weary hearts, whom the relentless hand of war had sorely stricken. All these were petitioners for something forbidden by the stern rules of cruel war. Our friends were approached by the colored messenger, to whom the lieutenant presented his card with the request that it be shown to the Secretary. It bore the names of Lieutenant Bedell, Eleventh Vermont Volunteers, and Mrs. Van Metre.

A number of applicants had already preceded them that morning. They expected to wait until all these had been presented to the Secretary. To their surprise the messenger immediately returned and said to them in a low voice: "The Secretary desires to see you at once. Follow me!"

They were conducted through one room into another. It was not that small, dark one with a railing across one corner, behind which the Secretary had stood so many times and dashed so many hopes to the earth by his curt "No! it can't be done!" but another, through the open door of which they saw a short man with glasses and a heavy beard seated at a desk, with huge piles of folded papers around and on every side of him.

As their names were announced and they were advancing with a slow and hesitating step, he sprang to his feet, came quickly forward to meet them, took the hand of the half-terrified woman in his warm and cordial grasp, and said in a voice which rang with its own clear sincerity:

"Madam, you are a noble woman, and it is a pleasure to meet you." Still holding her hand he continued: "You have met with a great misfortune, lieutenant, in the loss of your limb, but that loss was in some sense a blessing when it brought you such a friend."

Both were too much surprised to reply. Each felt that something ought to be said. Mrs. Van Metre first recovered herself and managed, with a broken voice scarcely above a whisper, to say: "But I am a Southern woman, Mr. Stanton."

"I know you are," he said, "and that is why your kindness to one of our wounded officers is such an act of charity—that greatest as it is the loveliest of all the virtues. I know that your husband is a Confederate soldier, and I hope he is as brave and true in his sphere as you are in yours. It is faint praise of you to say that you are an honor to your sex. I can and do say most sincerely that I wish every woman North and South would emulate your example. I do not ask you to be seated," he continued, "for here, in the pressure of business, I cannot converse with both of you as I wish. Besides, I have promised one of your sex, Mrs. Van Metre, for whom I have a high esteem, that she shall hear your story from your own lips. Will you both favor me with a call at my house about eight o'clock this evening?"

What could they say but yes? A quick movement of his hand indicated that their audience was over. In another moment this busiest of men was at his desk, buried beneath his ever-increasing mountain of public duties, and his visitors were shown to the street by another exit.

The lieutenant felt the hand of his companion trembling upon his arm, and he knew that behind her thick veil she was silently weeping tears, not of sorrow, but of gratitude. He made no observation until they reached their hotel and were about to separate. Then he said:

"I have great hopes of Secretary Stanton. I think he intends to assist us."

"And so have I," she replied. "God bless him! How different he is from what I supposed," she added fervently.

They separated, he enjoining her to compose herself for the evening. The lieutenant was surprised by the number of cards left for him, for he was yet to learn with what facility the representatives of the press may elevate a modest man to celebrity. Several of these gentlemen were waiting in the drawing-room to interview him, and their numbers were increasing. His natural good sense showed him, when they first assailed him with questions, that it would be unwise to open his lips until he had told his story to the Secretary and taken his advice. He undertook to maintain that position and to treat his inquisitors with civility. He supposed he had done so and that he had disclosed nothing about Mrs. Van Metre or himself, until he saw the evening journals. Then, to his astonishment, he saw his own portrait and one of Mrs. Van Metre, which was wholly imaginary, and under it an equally imaginary account of his recent experiences, which purported to have been written from his own dictation.

This experience was so disagreeable to the lieutenant and his charge that if so much had not depended on the friendship of Secretary Stanton, they would have invented some excuse for breaking their engagement to call upon him in the evening. But he left them no opportunity to escape. In the course of the afternoon a messenger brought them a note requesting them to be in readiness at an hour named, when a carriage would call to convey them to his residence. Obviously it was useless to contend against all the resources of the Government, and like sensible persons who had encountered an irresistible force, they submitted without farther resistance.

Their evening at the modest residence of Mr. Stanton on Franklin Square was memorable to themselves and a considerable number of ladies and gentlemen who were invited to meet them. They did not know until long afterward that the gathering comprised some of the most conspicuous representatives of European powers, as well as our own Republic. There were few introductions: there was such an absence of all formality and such cordiality was manifested by the ladies that Mrs. Van Metre lost her timidity and felt that she was among friends who sympathized with her in her trials. Nor was the experience of the lieutenant very difficult. Almost before he was conscious of the situation, he was eloquently relating the story of her energetic labors which had unquestionably saved his life. He was a plain man, this Vermonter, with a limited vocabulary and unpracticed in speech; but when he sketched the picture of that cheerless room where he lay deserted, helpless, and almost hoping for death, and told the story of her entrance, and how bravely she met the king of terrors, fought with and, notwithstanding all his advantages, finally defeated him in the long, fierce battle for the life of the wounded, helpless man; how she took him into her own despoiled home and by her cool bravery procured the means and by their skilful use finally saved him, the spell-bound company listened with breathless interest and their hearts were moved with the tenderest sympathy. Those who did not know him were accustomed to say that no tale of suffering could soften the flinty heart of the great war Secretary. Those who saw him that evening knew better, for at times it was evident that a considerable effort was necessary to enable him to suppress his emotions. A writer of eminence who was present declared that the pages of English literature held no story more touching, no clearer proof that truth was sometimes stranger than fiction. The voice, manner, and bearing of the narrator were a satisfactory test of the truth of his story.

The modest, brave wife, the preserver of the now strong and vigorous though crippled officer, was compelled to listen in silence to her own praises. The ladies vied with each other in their efforts to encourage and cheer her. They made her feel that although she was among the women of the North, she was surrounded with friends who would spare no exertions to serve her.

Lieutenant Bedell did not miss the opportunity to show to the Secretary the immediate and, for the time, the exclusive object of his life. It was to find the husband of his benefactress and restore him to his home. He related how he had parted from his own wife, who had willingly gone to his Vermont home that he might execute his search without anxiety on her account or that of his children. How far he succeeded in interesting those who then listened to his story the reader may infer from the parting words of his host. Holding both the hands of Mrs. Van Metre, now overcome by kindness and tremulous with emotion, he said:

"Madam, I know of nothing in the history of woman more meritorious than your conduct. We read in the Book of Books that 'a virtuous wife is a crown to her husband.' You are that and more—you are an honor to your country and your sex. I hope your trials are nearly over— that the order for his discharge has already reached your husband. If it has not, if you have any difficulty in finding him, the resources of my department will be prompt to assist you. You have earned the right to command them. Every gentleman in the service will, with me, esteem it an honor to assist you."

So they took their leave of the man she had so much feared, her heart full of the new hope which his kindness had inspired—of gratitude to the Almighty, who had shown her the path of duty and given her strength to follow it. That night she rested peacefully and the next morning awakened with renewed courage for the duty before her.

CHAPTER XXII.

THE FIRST FAILURE IN THE SEARCH.

The order for the release of Van Metre as a prisoner of war had been issued by the Secretary upon the theory that he was then confined in a certain camp of Confederate prisoners. His wife had not been greatly elated by the dispatch of the Secretary and the letter of General Hitchcock which had followed it, for if he was confined in that camp there was no explanation for his long silence. By the direction of the Secretary, Bedell prepared a paper giving a description of Van Metre. This paper was sent to the proper officer for a report. It came very promptly. It stated that Van Metre was captured in the valley in January, 1864, *that he had escaped, and that now there was no prisoner of that name whose name was borne on the records of the department.*

This report was a sore disappointment to the wife, but it was not unexpected to the lieutenant, who had constantly maintained that he would only be found after a long and weary search. He now proceeded to collect the facts concerning him, and these facts at once indicated that there was a good reason for Bedell's apprehension. Van Metre had enlisted in the regiment of cavalry raised in the valley, where he had been captured in January, 1864. On their way to Harper's Ferry his captors had, at his request, stopped at his house, permitted him to have an interview with his wife and to procure a change of clothing. He might easily have escaped from his guards, but would not because he had given them his word to that effect if they would permit him to call at his home. He had corresponded with his wife until the following May, since which time she had not heard from him. His last letter was from Camp Chase, at Columbus, Ohio, where he was taken at the time of his capture.

There was another rumor, altogether inconsistent with these facts. It was that on the 11th of May he had been among the captured at Spottsylvania Court-House, where, at the place afterward known as the "Bloody Angle," the Federal column swept down upon the division of General Edward Johnson and captured him with twenty pieces of artillery and twenty-eight hundred men. An acquaintance who was also captured and who afterward escaped reported that Van Metre was one of the prisoners and that he saw him when he was marched to the rear, apparently unwounded. From this time his wife had heard nothing of or from him.

When the report came from the veteran General Hitchcock, commissary-general of prisoners, that there was now no name of Van Metre upon the roll of Confederate prisoners, a very different effect was produced upon the two persons engaged in the search. The poor wife again felt the waves of despair overwhelming her. All her apprehensions returned, stronger than before she left the valley. Her husband must be dead, she thought; nothing but death would have prevented him from sending some message to her. There was no other way of accounting for his silence. She imagined many evils. He was bold, sometimes reckless. Naturally impatient under restraint—weary of the life of a prisoner, he had attempted to escape and had been shot down; or having made his escape he had sickened and died; or he had lost his life in some other way. These impressions, from which her mind had been relieved by its diversion to her care for Bedell, now returned with increased intensity. When the last report was received there was scarcely a gleam of hope in the dark horizon of her future.

This temporary obstruction instead of discouraging Bedell only inspired him to new exertions. When he put all the facts together, he promptly came to the conclusion that Van Metre's silence was in some way, he could not conceive how, connected with his escape. In spite of himself his mind continually recurred to his dream. He did not believe in dreams, of course. A man who did ought not to be suffered to go at large; he should be restrained, put out of harm's way like other lunatics. And yet that dream was curious and fearfully real. Was it not possible that having made his escape, Van Metre had determined to re-enlist in the Confederate service? Then it might have occurred to him that an escaped prisoner who re-enlisted, if captured again, before he was exchanged might be treated as a deserter if detected. He might have enlisted, therefore, under an assumed name or given a different name when he was again captured. There were many ways of accounting for the fact that he was still a prisoner, still living, and that his name did not appear upon the roll of prisoners.

Unable to work out a satisfactory conclusion in his own mind, he wisely decided to carry his problem to the Secretary of War. Instead of putting it aside, Mr. Stanton at once proffered any assistance he could give. "It has frequently happened," he said, "that captured men would not give their true names—the records of the office are not always reliable. It is by no means impossible that Van Metre is yet a prisoner." His advice was that before the taper of hope should be wholly extinguished in the heart of that sorrowing woman—before the search should be wholly abandoned, every depot of Confederate prisoners should be visited and every prisoner be examined. He would facilitate that search in every possible way. He would give Bedell and Mrs. Van Metre free transportation, permission to examine every prison, and an order on the officer in command to deliver to her any person whom she should claim as her husband.

And so it happened that Bedell went from the discouraged, almost heart-broken woman, with his own faith somewhat weakened, to the War Office; was there told that instead of giving up the search, he ought to regard it as only just begun; that in continuing it he was to have not only the countenance, but the actual interest of the War Office and its efficient head. The report of his consultation confirmed the purpose of Mrs. Van Metre not to give up while a ray of hope remained, and it was finally decided to prosecute the inquiry upon the new lines prescribed by the Secretary of War.

I suppose there will be readers of this book who will charge me with taking an unfair advantage if I here inject into it a little of "what I knew about Edwin M. Stanton." I am not indifferent to just criticism, but I shall risk even that to enable me to do an act of justice to this misjudged, misunderstood man.

I am perfectly aware that it was the prevailing opinion, especially among those who are wise to do evil but to do good have no knowledge, that Secretary Stanton was a cold, heartless, obstinate, cruel man, who delighted in inflicting pain and in adding insult to his refusals of favors which another would have granted. I knew the man better. I concede his brusque, sometimes rough manner. I neither excuse nor palliate this great defect. But it should be remembered that every day there was in his reception-room a large and varied crowd, many of whom were thieves—human vultures who would prey upon their country. These he detected by intuition and crushed by a sentence. Others were wives in search of their husbands, Rachels weeping for their children, all seeking passes through our lines or something else prohibited by the hard necessities of war. In many of their bosoms the last hope would be extinguished by his negative. He usually stood beside a desk or behind a railing upon which his arm rested with his head supported by his hand. No one who ever witnessed it could forget that sad procession. He disposed of the petitioners with rapidity. He heard enough of each to know that something was asked that could not be granted, when his curt refusal fell upon the hopes of the petitioner like the axe of the guillotine upon the neck of its victim. Very pitiable and very numerous were these scenes, and his seemed the only heart unmoved. There were some who saw him a few minutes after one of these sad receptions, where, when he was alone or only a friend was present, his stoicism gave way to all the emotions of pity and sympathy which filled his real, genuine heart. The lieutenant declared that his interviews with Mr. Stanton were sometimes closed by the cordial grasp of a hand upon which often a warm tear would fall after coursing along his thick, dark beard, even as the precious ointment that ran down upon the beard of Aaron went down to the skirts of his garments. Therefore it is that I do not doubt the statement that as often as the Secretary saw in the maimed officer the proof of what this Southern woman had done for a Northern soldier and heard the touching tale repeated he was deeply moved. I am unwilling to lose the opportunity, and sometimes create the occasion, of saying that I do personally know that Mr. Stanton was a kind, sympathetic, great-hearted American, as well as the great War Secretary.

With full authority from the Secretary to inspect all records and to prosecute the strictest search through every depot where there were any Confederate prisoners and an order to deliver to Mrs. Van Metre any person whom she should claim as her husband, the lieutenant next applied for assistance and advice to the commissary-general of prisoners. His story touched the gallant and venerable General Hitchcock as it had his chief, all the more intensely because he was himself a Vermonter, a descendant of Ethan Allen, whose name he bore. He was of the opinion that some one had blundered, and the available force of his office, with the assistance of Bedell, set about the work of ascertaining when and where the blunder was made, and of preparing a list of the depots of Confederate prisoners and the places where these prisoners were captured. Mrs. Van Metre, meanwhile, passed her time in assisting inquiry and in making new friends.

CHAPTER XXIII.

THE BLOODY ANGLE—THE PRISONER AND HIS BETRAYER.

WHEN in future times an American is tempted to the performance of an act which may tend to involve his country in civil war, may his good judgment counsel him to pause while he reads and reflects upon the story of the "Bloody Angle." Not in this book! Heaven forbid that I should shock its readers with a history which, after thirty years, I cannot read in the heat of a summer evening without a convulsive chill. It is with considerable hesitation that I give the slight sketch of it which my story seems to require.

The place which gained this sanguinary title was an angle of nearly ninety degrees in the line of the Confederate field defences, extending northward from Spottsylvania Court-House about one and one-half miles and then abruptly turned westward. On the 11th and 12th days of May, 1864, the two great generals of their time, each at the head of a powerful army of veteran soldiers, confronted each other on the plains of Virginia. Accident selected the field for the most terrible fighting of these armies, the most deadly combat which ever took place upon the western continent. It was just within and around the sharp corner in these Confederate works which projected northward and toward the Federal advance. Behind this angle was the division of Major-General Edward Johnson, numbering very nearly three thousand men and comprising twenty pieces of artillery. In front of it, about a half-mile away, was Hancock's command of the Union army, which comprised the divisions of Barlow and Birney.

I am perfectly aware that in the days when the short-sword of the Romans conquered the world, warriors necessarily fought to their death within its short length of each other; that there must have been very brave men who held the pass of Thermopylæ; that from the Assyrian invasion to the "charge of the light brigade" there have been hand-to-hand conflicts in many of the great battles of the world. But if on the face of this terrestrial globe there is any spot which has been the theatre of such a fierce, bloody, long-sustained, continuous contest as the Bloody Angle, I do not know where it is to be found nor in what volume its story has been recorded. Hand-to-hand fighting, not by scores or by companies, but by thousands—not by men accidentally thrown together, but by regiments and brigades deliberately marching to the shock;

cannon, their muzzles thrust through the crevices in the breastworks and there discharged, drawn back, reloaded, thrust forward, and fired over and over again; oaks of primeval growth literally gnawed to their fall by minié-balls, and in their fall crushing the combatants who were slaying each other beneath their shade; logs of breastworks splintered and broomed by swift missiles of death; dry trenches flowing with human blood; batteries of artillery with all their officers, men, and horses silent in death on the ground around the exploded caissons and disabled guns; the ground not merely covered, but piled four deep with the dead; the lines so close together that as the men fell forward the blue and the gray lay side by side or were piled in alternate layers; men dying in the act of stanching the mortal bayonet wounds only a moment before inflicted in the mad rage of battle —such were some of the sights and scenes of the Bloody Angle. Which party was the victor? Neither! Such men, of the same race, blood, and courage, fight and die—they may be crushed by overweight and overpowered by numbers, but they cannot be conquered. Such scenes may be imagined, but they cannot be painted nor described.

We are concerned only with the beginning of this conflict. Just as the dawn was struggling through the morning mists, Barlow and Birney, at the head of their respective divisions of Hancock's right wing of the Union army, in a dense column with a narrow front, rushed to the assault. They bounded over the works, and before the Confederates could recover from the shock, forced them back from their defences, encircled the division of General Edward Johnson as in a net of steel, and bore them to the number of twenty-eight hundred, with twenty guns, swiftly back to the Union rear. They were thus carried outside the storm which for the next twenty hours raged back and forth, like a hurricane in the waves of hell, over the Bloody Angle. During those hours the fate of the Confederacy was hanging in the balance. In a council of war the previous evening, General Grant had invited the opinions of his generals on the question whether the works could be carried and the Confederate line be broken at that place. A majority of the generals were of opinion that it could not. General Upton said: "I can capture the position and break their line. Whether the position can be held is a different question, which must depend upon the support given to the charging column." He led the charge successfully. But while charge after charge of the Confederates was defeated, the Union advance was checked and the Confederate line re-established but a short distance in the rear of the first. Then one body of trained soldiers was hurled against another with such force that both went down over and over again, until one of the commanders, it matters little which, weary of the expenditure of one of his own veterans to destroy a single veteran of his enemy, retired and left to the other the empty honor of holding the field. It was at the moment of one of the many Confederate charges of this day that General Lee rode up, clearly intending to make the charge by the side of General Gordon, who was to lead it. Then it was that the cry was raised by countless Confederate voices, "General Lee to the rear!" and a private soldier respectfully but firmly took the bridle-bit of the horse of his general and led him to a place of comparative safety.

The first sensations following his capture of a prisoner of war are seldom agreeable. Among the twenty-eight hundred of the captured was Van Metre, the husband of the woman of the valley. Although confident in his own mind that he had committed no impropriety, he was not certain that his captors would take so lenient a view of his case. He had placed himself under no obligation to the authorities at Camp Chase, it being his purpose to be left free to escape if he could by any means elude the vigilance of his guards. After a few weeks' experience there, he, in company with three others, made his escape, and after much suffering and danger had reached the army of Virginia only a few days before his second capture. He was a visitor to Johnson's division, and in fact on his way to his own regiment, which he supposed was in the vicinity of Staunton. He was therefore not a combatant. But he feared that if he was proved to have taken service, without being exchanged, in any other regiment than his own, he might, if again captured, be treated as a spy. He was a Confederate in every fibre—an intense Virginian, true to his flag. As no information of the circumstances of the assault had reached the prisoners, he with others supposed that they had been captured in a disreputable manner by a surprise. Almost without reflection, he determined that the safest course for him would be to suppress his name and regiment. He was, under the circumstances, naturally thoughtless and irritable. When it was proposed to the prisoners that in consideration of liberties to be allowed them they should promise, for the time, not to attempt to escape, he peremptorily refused to give any pledge and declared that he intended to regain his liberty at the first opportunity. When they were asked to give their names and regiments he made no answer. Another prisoner who claimed to know him invented a name and a regiment for him. He was regarded as contumacious and, with a few others equally uncompromising, was separated from the mass of the prisoners, marched by the shortest route to the

Potomac, ferried across to Point Lookout, dropped into the multitude of thousands of Confederate prisoners as "John Thompson, First Arkansas Cavalry," and, except as a prisoner who had escaped from Camp Chase, his true name no longer appeared upon any Federal record of Confederate prisoners.

From this time misfortunes accumulated upon the head of the unfortunate prisoner known by the name of John Thompson. He was naturally conscientious and would have recoiled from the thought of intentional misrepresentation. But now he was brought to a sense of his true situation. In a moment of thoughtless irritation he had forfeited his name and his claim to the rights of a prisoner of war. He condemned his own conduct unsparingly, began to look upon his misfortunes as no more than he deserved, but for the time could discover no way of amending his situation.

From its commencement, his imprisonment at Point Lookout was more intolerable than his previous experience at Camp Chase. The location of the camp was solitary and depressing, and one feature of it was especially objectionable and annoying. The large number of prisoners were guarded exclusively by colored regiments almost wholly made up of emancipated slaves, who were held in contempt, as inferiors, by the Confederates but recently their masters, who in turn made use of their temporary authority, too often in the most offensive manner. The men sent with Van Metre to Point Lookout proved to be the most disreputable creatures in the service, with whom he could have no association. His remorse and self-condemnation, with the unhealthy condition of the camp, produced a condition of physical weakness which increased his irritability and made him peculiarly susceptible to annoyances which would not have disturbed a healthy man.

What was he to do? He now appreciated that he ought to have given his true name to his captors and to have announced that he was an escaped prisoner, on his way to join his own regiment when he was captured; that he was temporarily with, but not attached to, Johnson's command. This duty he had neglected at the proper time when it should have been done. He could discover no practicable way of repairing his error. He was surrounded by ignorant guards; there was no one with whom he could consult; every day's delay seemed to render it more and more difficult for him to restore himself to the position he would have occupied if he had not suppressed his true name. He deemed it hazardous to attempt to communicate with his wife or with any one else under his assumed name; to do so under his true name would involve an explanation with consequences which he feared might subject him to trial and condemnation by a court-martial.

In this condition of uncertainty he passed several weeks. The number of prisoners at Point Lookout increased with every great battle, but none came from the valley—all were from other sections of the Confederacy and strangers to him. As the autumn rains came on, a type of fever began to prevail in the camp, and Van Metre was one of the first to be attacked. He fought against it as long and as well as he could, but toward the end of October he gave up, took to his bed, and in a few days was ordered to be transferred to that section of the camp which was called the hospital.

There was then employed as a nurse in the fever ward of the hospital one of those creatures generated only by war or some other diseased condition of the public mind. He was probably more despicable than was ever covered by a colored skin, or found elsewhere than in a prison camp. He would have sold himself for any one, even the smallest, of the thirty pieces paid to Judas. A bounty-jumper who had enlisted and deserted more times than was safe at the North, he had then enlisted with the Confederates, been captured, and was now seeking to ingratiate himself with the officers at Point Lookout by playing the character of a voluntary pimp and spy. Taking advantage of Van Metre's weak condition and his strong desire for the counsel and sympathy of a man of his own color, this wretch had adroitly wormed himself into his confidence, ascertained his real name and regiment, his escape from Camp Chase, his success in reaching the army of Virginia on his way to his own regiment, then supposed to be near Staunton or Harrisonburg. He had volunteered, for a compensation, to mail a letter which Van Metre was extremely desirous of sending to his wife. Knowing that, unless surreptitiously, no letter could leave the camp written by him under any other name than that of Thompson, he had paid the fellow his last coin to deposit a letter to his wife in his own name. Such a letter would then have reached Mrs. Van Metre, for at that time Clarke County, where she resided, was within the Union lines. The wretch pocketed the bribe, carried the letter to the officer in command of the post, and informed him that the writer was a Confederate spy whose name was Van Metre. That officer having ascertained that Van Metre was too ill at that time to do any harm or to attempt to escape, contented himself with increased watchfulness over him, and at the same time extended that watchfulness to the informer, whose good faith was soon brought under vehement suspicion.

The prisoner very soon discovered how basely he had been cheated and betrayed. He was then in the delirious stage of the fever, and but for a fortunate accident would probably never have recovered the exercise of his reason. With the singular secretiveness sometimes exhibited by the insane, he concealed his suspicions, suppressed his resentment, and even professed to bestow upon the creature an increased measure of confidence and friendship. In some way never disclosed, and which the officers did not exhibit a very irrepressible desire to investigate, he possessed himself of one of the heavy rawhides wielded by the army teamsters in the process of disciplining refractory mules. For many days he kept the weapon concealed in his cot under his body. The day of retribution came, when Providence delivered the scoundrel into the hands of his victim. There was no one to molest or make him afraid. The guards outside, ordinarily quick to come at any unaccustomed sound, were that day unaccountably deaf. It was no part of the duty of the patients in the ward to interfere. Van Metre rose from his cot, and as no one sought to prevent him, so long as his strength held out he scored his revenge in red, swollen ridges and bloody welts upon the face, neck, chest, and shoulders of his betrayer. Then he went back to his cot, with his strength exhausted, in the frenzy of brain fever, and for many days was mercifully unconscious of his surroundings.

Then his naturally vigorous constitution was

left to fight the battle for life against the combined forces of disease, imprisonment, and negligence without outside interference. One hour he was burning with fever, the next his lips were blue and his teeth rattling with convulsive chills. The carelessness of human life, the gross negligence involved, may be imperfectly comprehended by the fact that when the stripes of his castigation were healed, the malicious bounty-jumper and detective fraud was permitted to return and have charge of the ward in which Van Metre suffered. His infamous brain conceived the project of destroying the helpless prisoner by neglect and exposure. Under the lying pretext that he was dangerous in his madness, iron shackles were locked upon his wrists and ankles, and his body became the feeding-ground of parasites and vermin. His accursed ingenuity in devising new methods of torture would have done credit to an Indian. I will not shock the nerves of the reader by any further account of his devilish devices. They operated slowly, but with a certainty and a keenness of suffering that would have shocked the sensibilities of the monster who made Andersonville celebrated as the theatre of his crimes and the scene of his final punishment.

CHAPTER XXIV.

"WHAT I DID FOR HIM I THOUGHT SOME NORTHERN WOMAN MIGHT DO FOR MY HUSBAND."

THOSE who were accustomed to visit the hospitals during the battle summer of 1864, among their memories of pain, suffering, and death will recall one delightful picture. It was that of woman, with the crown royal, arrayed like Vashti the queen to show the people her beauty. She was met in every ward, in every hospital, in the early morning, at midday, and at midnight. She represented every station in life: wealthy ladies who spent all their time and more than their income in relieving the pain and torture of the sick and wounded; wives of mechanics and laboring men; colored women, old and young, very poor in this world's goods, but not so poor that each one could not bring a basket of delicacies to distribute to the patients; the Sisters of Charity, those efficient Catholic nurses whose quiet influence pervaded the fever wards and controlled the delirium of the fever-stricken—all these and others, many others, were found constantly employed in some work of charity, some mission of relief to suffering men.

There were a few of these ladies whose influence was exercised over a broader stage. These went from camp to camp, from hospital to hospital, searching out and correcting frauds and abuses. These last were the special favorites of Secretary Stanton and could always count upon his co-operation. They were as cordially disliked by unfaithful managers of these institutions, who were in many instances brought to justice through their influence.

There was a veteran general whose fighting days were ended in the war with Mexico, whose name had long been on the retired list, but who still retained some capacity for work, which he desired to employ in some manner in the service of his country. He had offered his services to Secretary Stanton, who, with that excellent judgment which he usually showed in the selection of men for positions of difficulty, promptly accepted his offer and requested him to visit, inspect, and report upon the camps where the Confederate prisoners of war were confined. The general was admirably adapted to such a responsible duty, which required good judgment and a sharp eye not to be deceived by preparations in anticipation of a visit of inspection.

This officer had a daughter who inherited her father's energy and many other of his excellent qualities. Her husband, a brave general of division, had fallen in the supreme moment of a great battle in 1862. Instead of yielding to so great a sorrow, she had risen above it and determined to continue, so far as she could, that service to the country which her brave husband could no longer render. She had become her father's secretary, his constant attendant on his tours of inspection, and had become very efficient in the discharge of her duties. It was impossible to conceal from the sharp eyes of this father and daughter any evidences of negligence or inattention to duty. They were the terror of unfaithful superintendents. On the most unexpected occasions they would suddenly make their appearance, to the great profit and advantage of the prisoners and the dismay of incompetent officials.

The demonstration of General Early against the city of Washington and its narrow escape from capture in July, 1864, had sharply called public attention to the condition of the prisoners' camp at Point Lookout. The existence of this camp had not been regarded as important. But when General Bradley Johnson, with five thousand cavalrymen, was detached from Early's army on the Monocacy and sent to cut the railroads north of Baltimore, and was rapidly approaching a camp of twenty thousand healthy prisoners, guarded only by two colored regiments which had never been in battle, the North was suddenly aroused to the magnitude of the danger. But for the arrival of two divisions of the Sixth Corps at Washington, which compelled General Early to recall General Johnson and make a hasty retreat across the Potomac, the camp at Point Lookout would almost certainly have been captured and its twenty thousand recruits have been furnished to the army of General Lee, free of the cost of exchange.

Soon after the retreat of General Early many of the prisoners at Point Lookout were sent to other camps. The active movements of the army before Richmond, followed by Sheridan's campaign in the valley, attracted public attention to other points, and Point Lookout came to be regarded as of no special importance. It thus became one of the places where the experience of the veteran inspector had shown that abuses would rapidly develop which would require his attention.

Toward the middle of November, the general and his daughter made their unexpected appearance in the camp at Point Lookout. They swept through all its departments with a rapidity which gave the officers in charge no time to get ready. They met even upon their cursory inspection with a succession of shocks and surprises. Since the distribution of the prisoners to other camps in July, this depot had received large additions of prisoners from the field, and the number was now too large for the force of attendants and guards. But there was no excuse for the existing filth, and evidences of neglect of duty were overwhelming. The guards had apparently used reasonable diligence to prevent the escape of the prisoners, and had then left them to take care of themselves. It had never been the policy of the Government to neglect its prisoners. Good food in abundance, clothing, medicines, and medical attendance were supposed to be everywhere provided. Regulations required that every part of the camp should be policed daily, and under all circumstances all the conditions of health were directed to be observed and secured. The lady continued her investigations after the first cursory inspection was completed. She had been disgusted by that inspection. It was evident that no attention had been given to the regulations and no attempt made to enforce them. Her dissatisfaction rose to fever heat when she entered the hospitals, which her father had not yet seen. It increased as she passed rapidly through the wards. She had not reached the last one when she decided to suspend her inspection until she could have the judgment of her father and his friend and associate.

For the veteran general had a friend very much after his own heart who was a veteran surgeon. He stood at the head of his profession when he retired from active practice, and had been pleased to accept the invitation of his old military friend to accompany him on his inspections and assist him in relieving the suffering men whom the chances of war had for the time being made our prisoners.

The father and his surgical expert were pressed by the daughter to complete their inspection of the camp and the hospitals without another hour's delay. They complied, first insisting upon the attendance of the surgeon in charge. He came. They demanded to know whether the stench, which almost overpowered them as they entered the first inclosure where prisoners were confined, was an indispensable necessity. The surgeon in charge undertook to explain it. He said it was due to the laziness of the prisoners, who would not keep their quarters in a cleanly condition. The prisoners furiously denied this statement, and offered to clean their quarters at once, if furnished with the necessary materials and permitted to procure their own water, which they had not been allowed to do. The inspecting party went through the camp, and within an hour almost every prisoner was engaged in cleaning his person or his quarters. This reform, so easily instituted, was made permanent by the prompt removal of the surgeon, and its beneficial effects continued until peace dispensed with the necessity of any camp for prisoners of war.

The hour was so late that it was deemed necessary to postpone the visit to the fever wards until the following day. The delay was vehemently objected to by the daughter, on the ground that it would cost the lives of some of the patients she had already seen. Her associates did not believe that there was any foundation for her fears: they were of a different opinion before their inspection was completed.

When they visited the hospitals next morning a single glance showed that they were an affront to the name. They were extensive. Disease had been prevalent; it had been spread by neglect and the patients were counted by hundreds. The indignation of the party grew hotter as they progressed, for each ward seemed filthier than the last they had passed through. They entered what were called the fever wards. The fever was prevalent and almost every patient was delirious. The fetid atmosphere, the horrible expressions of insanity made the place resemble the incurable wards of a mad-house. It was a hard trial for the lady to endure; but she would not retreat. I shall spare my readers the horrors of the picture which met their astonished eyes. She finally led them to a room at which she had taken a hasty glance the night before.

It was crowded with cots, in every one of which lay a fever-stricken man. In one of them, upon a bed of straw, reeking with filth, in underclothing which had not been changed for months, were the almost fleshless remains of what had once been a healthy man. His hollow, sunken eyes were wild with the insane fire of fever, which was burning up the strength and consuming the juices of his body. The grime of his face could not conceal its ashen pallor; his beard, the growth of months, and his matted hair were alive with unmentionable vermin. His parched lips, seamed with bloody cracks, opened with difficulty, and as he saw them looking at the name over his head, his weak voice struggled to say: "No! no! Not Thompson! My name is Van Metre!"

The general had to put forth all his energy to maintain his self-control. Turning to the surgeon of the camp, he demanded in a voice which was piercing in its intensity: "Where is the man who is responsible for the care of this prisoner?"

A wretch with the mouth of a rat and the general expression of a hyena, every feature of whose face was vile, had been chattering in the rear of the party that the man was insane; that he had tried to kill his attendants; that he would not obey their directions; that it had been necessary to restrain him, etc. He was pointed out to the visitors as the nurse.

The general called for a sergeant and a file of men. As soon as they came he said: "Put that man under guard in a safe place. If necessary put him in irons. Let him escape at your peril! There—take him away!"

He was obeyed. By the suggestion of his consulting surgeon he ordered a tent to be prepared in the only shaded place in the vicinity. Very tenderly was poor Van Metre placed upon a stretcher and carried to a bath-room, where by the administration of stimulants, with great care the grime and filth were removed from his body, his head and face were shaved and their living tenants were extirpated. Then he was carried to the tent, provided with underclothing, and placed between clean sheets on a soft mattress. Strengthening restoratives were administered and a regimen prescribed which secured him a repose of several hours.

Notwithstanding his fortunate discovery by the efficient relief party, the condition of Van Metre continued to be very precarious. The exertion of his necessary ablution and of cleansing him from the grime which coated his person, followed by the exhaustion of a long and profound sleep, produced a succession of fainting fits which could only be arrested by powerful stimulants. The veteran surgeon advised the employment of an experienced nurse who would not relax his vigilance for a moment, for the neglect of that moment might prove fatal. Such a nurse was found with less difficulty than the surgeon anticipated. The sympathies of the general's daughter had been powerfully excited by the sufferings of the prisoner and the brutality of his attendant. With a firmness not unlike that shown by Mrs. Van Metre on her first visit to the room of the wounded and deserted officer, and it may have been for a like cause, she announced her purpose to become the nurse of the maltreated prisoner and the guide of his trembling steps on the road to convalescence. Neither the surgeon nor her father remonstrated, for a human life was involved. The former prepared the remedies which were to be administered whenever the patient awoke to consciousness. She took her seat by his bedside and commenced a vigil of watchfulness which was not relaxed until the patient was declared free from immediate danger.

CHAPTER XXV.

AND THE RECOMPENSE OF A MAN'S HANDS SHALL BE RENDERED UNTO HIM.

In the last year of the war there were deaths from wounds so slight that they scarcely attracted attention until their fatal character was established. There were other cases of recovery from wounds so severe that they went far toward establishing the claims of those who believed in faith cures and miraculous interpositions. In the cases first named, the patient was depressed, hopeless, indifferent whether he lived or died; in the second, he was either cheered by hope or encouraged by duty. A wounded soldier among strangers, suffering an agony of pain, treated as if he were an animal or a machine, with no one to care for or sympathize with him, would often welcome death as a deliverer and a friend, when the same man upon the appearance in the hospital of a wife, a sister, or even of a stranger who sympathized with him or took some interest in his recovery, at once lifted him out of his despondency and placed him in the way to health and convalescence.

The influence upon Van Metre of the unremitting care of his volunteer nurse, and especially her avowed purpose to watch him closely, to secure for him every advantage, and see that he lost no opportunity of improvement, was most favorable. And there was another occurrence about the same time which multiplied his favorable chances. His betrayer was brought into his presence, and there occurred a scene which very closely resembled the one witnessed by Bedell in his dream, which it will be remembered was by him related to Mrs. Van Metre when he was first taken to her home. The fact that the knavery of his betrayer had been detected by strangers without his intervention, and the prospect that the criminal would be brought to justice and punished, planted a new hope in his mind that he might live and witness the infliction of that punishment. But there could have been no substitute for the untiring industry of the general's daughter. The veteran surgeon had prepared the stimulating remedies he prescribed with his own hands. They were to be administered as often as the patient showed any signs of waking. The general's daughter then seated herself by the bedside of the patient; the remedies were within reach of her hand. A trained nurse was in the adjoining room within her call. There she kept her faithful watch, administering as often as every hour some refreshing or stimulating remedy, until by the second morning the strength of the patient was unexpectedly increased, his condition was more promising than the surgeon had anticipated, and he was declared to be on the high-road to recovery.

The experience of Van Metre bore a close resemblance to that of Bedell in another respect. Bedell was no more confident that he was preserved from death by the ministrations of Mrs. Van Metre during the first night after his discovery by her, than Van Metre was that he owed his life to the watchful nursing of the general's daughter during the night following his removal from the hospital ward to the tent at Point Lookout. He was in truth reduced to the last degree of weakness. A few hours more of that murderous, intentional negligence, and nothing short of a miracle could have saved him. The flame of his life was flickering so feebly that a breath would have extinguished it. The exhaustion of his first sleep would have been fatal but for the judgment and watchful care of his nurse and her strict observance of the directions of the veteran surgeon.

He was now moderately certain of recovery if the danger of a relapse could be avoided. Nothing but incessant care could prevent such a misfortune, but of that care he was now assured. Although he was no longer tortured by the wild images of delirium, reason did not immediately resume her full empire over his mind. His memory was more impaired than his other mental powers; sometimes it seemed wholly lost, and then his efforts to recall past events were painful to witness. He seemed to be aware that he had done some wrong—something for which he was liable to punishment, but what it was he could not recall. He made desperate efforts to remember it, and failing believed he had become idiotic. These efforts were a heavy tax upon his vitality, and his nurse labored diligently to prevent their recurrence.

At length a morning came when he was able to remember the past and to comprehend his present. His nurse, relieved from the necessity of continuous attendance, was paying him a visit. Her interest in his recovery was unabated and her visits sufficiently frequent to secure him against farther inattention.

"I have a confession to make to you," he said to her. "I fear you will have no faith in me after you have heard it. But I have suffered enough by deception. Now I wish to have every one know the truth."

"There is an old saying that confession is good for the soul," she replied. "However, I do not see how you, a prisoner, could have committed any offence while you have been sick and in prison. Of what do you accuse yourself?"

"Of permitting others to misrepresent me and not correcting them," he said. "My name is not

Thompson. It is Van Metre, and I am an escaped prisoner. But I am not a spy, as that villain who had control of me falsely stated."

"What of all that? To pass by a false name may be deception, but it is no crime. What gave you such an idea?"

"I was a prisoner, confined at Camp Chase in Columbus, Ohio. With a number of other prisoners I escaped, as I suppose I had the right to do. Those who got away from the prison separated. After many hardships, almost naked and starved, I reached the army of General Lee before Richmond, on my way to my own regiment, which I supposed was somewhere in the upper portion of the valley. I had not joined any regiment since my escape. If I had done so without being exchanged I suppose I should have been subject to punishment. I permitted another prisoner to give a false name for mine because I feared that, finding me with Johnson's division, I should be treated and punished as having joined it. Since my confinement here I have written a letter in my true name to my wife, which the villain who had charge of me was hired to mail. Instead of mailing, he delivered it to the officer in command of this post, and told him a lot of lies about my being a Confederate spy. I assure you that I have done no other wrong."

"I do not believe you are guilty of any offence whatever," said the spirited woman. "If you are, it cannot be one of much account. You have done right in disclosing it to me. I will consult my father, who will advise you wisely and I am certain will stand your friend. In the mean time is there anything farther that I can do for you?"

"Yes. There is one very great favor which I fear will not be granted until my miserable deception is cleared up. In all these five months my poor wife near Berryville has not heard from me, nor have I had any message from her. She must think that I am dead or, what is worse, that I have forgotten or abandoned her. If the officer in command of this station would permit me to write her a brief letter, telling her that I am living and explaining why she has not heard from me during this long and weary time, I would ask no other favor. Poor woman! she is in my mind every hour and every moment when I am in control of my senses."

"There is no reason of which I can conceive why you should not have such a letter written and forwarded to-day," she said. The assurance relieved his fears and produced upon his despondent mental condition a better effect than medicine. As soon as the facts were communicated to him, the officer in command of the camp promptly consented that the fact of the prisoner's existence, condition, and place of confinement should be made known to his wife by letter addressed to her *via* Harper's Ferry. The letter was written and mailed. It reached Harper's Ferry without any delay, but the Union army had been withdrawn and the region around Berryville was again under Confederate control. The letter accordingly remained in the post-office at Harper's Ferry, undelivered. At the time Mrs. Van Metre and Bedell were arranging to begin their search, this letter, which would have relieved their anxieties and informed them where Van Metre was, lay in the post-office at Harper's Ferry, where they then were. They had no knowledge of it, and so far as they were concerned it might just as well have been at the north pole.

The small but efficient party of inspection, which might well have been called a relief party, knew that in such a camp the fatality was largely due to mental causes, and they devoted themselves to schemes and plans for the occupation of the minds of the prisoners. Van Metre had his full share of their attention. They encouraged him with the hope of his own recovery, of again seeing his home and his wife, who would have her solicitude relieved by his letter, and would probably within a few days transmit her reply. The general farther increased his chances of recovery by pointing out to him that his evidence would be necessary to convict his villanous guard, whom he proposed to bring to trial before a court-martial. His duty to bring that wretch to justice, and the hope which these encouragements brought to a heart from which it had long been absent, gave the mind of the patient constant and healthful occupation, until other duties called the general and his skilful associates to other fields of usefulness.

They left the camp before their patient had gained such a measure of physical strength that unassisted nature could accomplish his cure. The surroundings of the place became more depressing with the approach of winter. The camp was on a low and narrow peninsula, with a broad marsh on one side and the river on the other. There was not a hill, there was scarcely a human dwelling near it. There were a few trees on the slight elevation where his tent was pitched, but no other vegetation except that of the marshes in view. His removal to the tent, of which he was the only occupant, from the close and crowded wards of the shed dignified with the name of the hospital, and the excellent care which he continued to receive, would have protected him against a relapse if he had not been previously reduced to a degree of weakness which was very near to death. The general's daughter exercised a powerful influence over him. For some days after her departure he lived upon her memory and managed to bear himself fairly well. But as day followed day and one long night followed another, and no reply came to his letter, no news from his home, no message from his wife, having no one to lean upon and left wholly to his own resources, he began to lose the strength he had gained. There is no depression to which man can be subjected so disheartening as that which accompanies the weakness of fever. The dark cloud which obscures the vision shuts out all hope, all light. It is then that the patient needs all his conscience, all his moral principle, for the devil never leaves him—never ceases to whisper in his ear: "Why do you continue to suffer? You have become worthless—good for nothing for yourself or others! Why not avail yourself of suicide, your best, your only friend?"

It was a time of great mortality in that crowded camp. The dense fogs which every morning ascended from the broad marsh were laden with malaria. An active fever became prevalent which struck down its victims within two or three days from the first attack. From his cot through the door of his tent, every morning Van Metre witnessed the long procession moving from the hospital toward the piece of flat marsh which had been inclosed by a rude fence and called the cemetery, where men were laid in ditches without prayer or other ceremony. Finally he gave up all hope of recovery and looked forward to the day, which could not be far distant, when he himself would be one of those borne in that long and dreary procession. Leaving him in this desponding condition, our history returns to those who were now to test the verity of the promise, "Seek and ye shall find!"

CHAPTER XXVI.

"I HAVE NOT FOUND SO GREAT FAITH; NO, NOT IN ISRAEL."

The fact that according to the records Van Metre was no longer a prisoner nor under the control of the Federal authorities might have discouraged a less determined man, but it served to inspire Bedell with a fiercer resolution. He repeated to himself over and over again that only fools and old women believed in dreams. Yet that dream of his implied that Van Metre was still a prisoner—that he had been very ill—that he was then in good hands and recovering. . He counted the dream as worthless rubbish, but at the same time it led him to adhere to his determination formed upon all the facts and circumstances, as soon as he learned that his name was not on the list of prisoners, that he would not abandon the search until he had found Van Metre or inspected every prisoner of war who then remained under Federal control.

The officers in charge of the Bureau of Prisoners at Washington entered upon the subject of the search with great interest. In fact their zeal, excited by the pathetic face and gentle dignity of the wife, led them astray and protracted the search. Had they directed Bedell in the first instance to the camp where the largest number of prisoners captured by the Army of the Potomac in the campaign of 1864 had been sent, and where presumptively the chances of finding his man would have been best, they would have found him in the first camp examined, in the tent at Point Lookout.

He had been sent, as the records showed, to Camp Chase at the time of his original capture. Although his escape from that camp was reported, he might have been recaptured or his pursuers might have got some trace of him which would indicate where he was or otherwise assist in the search. They did not altogether discredit the indefinite rumor that he had been seen among the captured of General Johnson's division near Spottsylvania. Those prisoners had been distributed to different camps; some of them to Camp Chase. On the whole, it was decided that Camp Chase was the best point for commencing the search.

Provided with transportation and armed with all the authority and facilities which the War Department could furnish, Mrs. Van Metre and her escort set out upon their search. There were several camps to be examined, some of them containing as many as twenty thousand captives, for up to that time no general exchange of priscners had been arranged, and some one was morally responsible for thousands of lives lost by the delay. It was no child's play to examine the face of every individual in one of these multitudes. For the plan upon which Bedell insisted involved also the inspection of every cot in the hospitals and of every name in the records of the dead. Every facility and assistance was rendered by the authorities at most of the camps. Commencing at Camp Chase, a station was provided, the men were turned out in detachments and in single file slowly marched past the searchers, who were thus able to scrutinize every face. This done, they went through every ward and examined every patient in the hospital, completing their work by a close inspection of the records of the dead. This work occupied several days in each camp, and it was thoroughly done.

And so they went from camp to camp performing their sad, monotonous duty. They had performed it in most of them; only two or three remained to be examined. By the persistent encouragement of Bedell, the hope and courage of the patient wife had been fairly well maintained. But now her strength was yielding, and as these many days of patient search produced nothing, her hope and courage were failing with her strength. They were just completing a tour in a hospital, the last thing to be done in one of the large camps, when she began to hang with her full weight upon the arm of her escort, and then she sank wearied and fainting to the floor.

They laid her upon an unoccupied cot; the attendants gathered about her and endeavored to restore her by the use of the common remedies in such cases. All were attracted by the refined expression of her face, and in answer to an inquiry Lieutenant Bedell mentioned her name. It reached the ear of a sick man in an adjacent cot.

"Who is that lady?" he abruptly asked of his attendant.

"She is a lady from the valley of Virginia," replied the attendant. "Her husband was a soldier in the Confederate army who has been captured and if living is now a prisoner. She has not heard from him in many months. On account of some kindness she has shown to a Union officer, the Secretary of War has given her an order for the discharge of her husband and authorized her to search for him through all the camps. She expected to find him here. She has not found him and now it is almost certain that he is dead. We all feel very sorry for her, for she is a very sweet woman and must be dreadfully disappointed. They say that she saved the life of the Union officer who is with her."

"Did I not hear some one call her Mrs. Van Metre?" asked the sick man.

"Yes. Her name is Van Metre," said the

nurse. "There is some doubt about the place where her husband was captured. He was first captured near Front Royal, in the valley: there is also a rumor that he was taken with Johnson's division in the great battle near Spottsylvania Court-House."

"Van Metre? Van Metre?" exclaimed the sick man. "If I were not so weak and forgetful I am almost certain that I could tell that lady something about her husband. Let me think!" he continued. "Yes! it was after we were taken at Spottsylvania; and there was some trouble. If the lady remains here over night I will try and think how it was."

To fly to the sorrowing wife and relight the dying taper of hope in her heart by telling her that here was one who possibly knew something about her husband, was the loving mission of the nurse. For everywhere the gentle woman and her noble though crippled escort went, they made friends who wished to enlist in their service. Bedell immediately consulted with the surgeon, who directed them to be very cautious with the sick man. He had been delirious, was still very weak, and excitement might cause a return of his fever with all its dangerous symptoms. The surgeon took a deep interest in the matter, and offered himself not only to get the man into a condition for the exercise of his memory, but to draw the story from him in its most authentic form.

Bedell and Mrs. Van Metre, while burning with impatience to hear the sick man's story, recognized the wisdom of the doctor's advice. Their solicitude was so great that neither of them slept during the night, which seemed to both one of the longest they had ever passed.

In the morning the patient was reported to be in his right mind. He insisted upon the presence of Mrs. Van Metre with the surgeon, and in a very weak voice but with a memory apparently very clear he made the following communication:

He belonged, he said, to Johnson's division. He distinctly remembered a man who strongly resisted capture on the ground that he did not belong to the division and was a non-combatant who was present by accident. When the division was carried to the Union rear, this man was in or near the centre of the mass of men, and before he could make his way to the outside they were a long way within the Union lines. Even then he made an attempt to burst through the strong line of the guards—was seized by two or three of them and threatened with violence if he did not submit. He gave up when overpowered by main force, but when required to pledge himself to go with the others quietly farther to the rear, refused to make any promise, and said he should endeavor to make his escape at the first opportunity. An officer undertook to reason with him, and to show him that by farther efforts he might compel them to do him some great personal injury. He endeavored to make him promise to march quietly back with the others until they were turned over to the commissary.

He would make no promise. He told the officer that it might be better for him to die then and there than to lead the life of a prisoner. When the names and regiments of the others were taken, he said he did not belong to any regiment and would give no name. Some one of the prisoners said his name was John Thompson, of some Arkansas regiment. When asked if that was his name, he replied, "That name will do as well as any other." When the body of the prisoners moved on, he was left with four or five others under a special guard. The sick man heard that his name was Van Metre and that his home was in the valley. So much he learned from men who claimed to know him.

This was all the patient personally knew. He heard afterward that Van Metre was believed to be insane, and with a small number of others equally unmanageable had been sent directly across the river to Point Lookout, to a large camp of Confederate prisoners.

While this account was rather incoherent and wholly failed to furnish any information as to Van Metre's present locality, it nevertheless, if it were true, proved that he had reached the army after his escape from Camp Chase, and had been again taken prisoner at Spottsylvania. It thus gave them a new starting-point in the search. Bedell was much more hopeful than his associate. She did not place much confidence in the sick man's report, though she joyfully accepted it as the first evidence which she had secured that her husband was living at so late a period as the battle of Spottsylvania. They were then nearly four hundred miles away from Point Lookout, and they traversed the distance as swiftly as they could be transported by the power of steam. Bedell was now confident of success and so sanguine that he succeeded in imparting some of his confidence to his dejected travelling companion.

Even this small measure of success was fortunate. In any enterprise of difficulty, vigorous health and a hopeful temperament are the best equipment. More than once the discouraged wife would have given up the search but for Bedell, and now just when they were approaching success, one who lacked his push and energy would have been driven from the track by official incapacity. For when they reached Camp Lookout, the wife worn down by her exertions and almost overcome by depression, they found it the largest they had encountered, and that the inspection of twenty thousand men would be a long and fatiguing task. The officer in charge, unacquainted with the circumstances, took only a perfunctory interest in the work. He did not intend to disobey the Secretary's order, he said. There the prisoners were, twenty thousand of them. They could examine them at their pleasure. He did not intend to interfere with or take any responsibility for the proceeding.

There was a report current at the time that his indifference raised the indignation of the Green Mountaineer to concert pitch. He informed the officer that unless he facilitated the examination by ordering the prisoners to be brought out in detachments and marched in single file past Mrs. Van Metre, so that she could plainly see the face of every one of them, he would go directly to Secretary Stanton and let him know with how little respect his order was treated. He had an impression, he said, that the Secretary would find a way to interest that officer in the search.

The emphasis with which Bedell declared his purpose and his familiar reference to Secretary Stanton, who was a special terror to the "how-not-to-do-it" subordinates of the War Department, proved effective. The officer in command made a virtue of necessity and declared that he would do anything within the bounds of reason that Bedell requested. It is due to him to say that no complaint could have been made of his subsequent conduct in the premises.

Under the lieutenant's active supervision arrangements were made for a very thorough search. A tent was pitched in a convenient place in which Mrs. Van Metre could sit and see every face in succession, without being herself exposed to the public gaze, while the prisoners in single file were slowly marching by. The arrangements occupied the short December day, and the movement of the prisoners was necessarily postponed until the following morning.

When the morning came it seemed as though nature was conspiring with the evils of war to tax this burdened wife beyond her power to endure. She had passed a sleepless, restless night. The morning was inexpressibly dreary. A thick, chilling fog covered the camp and its surroundings, shutting out the rays and warmth of the sun. Her strength and her hope were both exhausted. Bedell knew how to inspire her to the last exertion of which she was capable. It was by an appeal to her sense of duty. He had been long enough a soldier to know what above all other remedies would restore strength to the exhausted body. With his own hands he prepared her breakfast of coffee and crackers, and pointed out to her that she must by their use strengthen herself for a duty that might have her husband for its reward. She responded as well as she could. Under the influence of the benignant draught she walked to the raised platform just inside the tent used for the purpose of the review, seated herself upon it, and the long procession began its movement.

When the first prisoner appeared she looked into his face with eager eyes, for then her strength and her hope were both at their highest level. She knew that her trial would occupy several hours. She had striven with all her resolution to qualify herself to endure it. One by one—one by one, for those long and weary hours, the slow funereal procession moved on. Like the brave, true woman she was, she summoned all her strength to maintain her composure and her hope. The lieutenant bravely continued to encourage and sustain her with cheerful suggestions and hopeful counsels. But the trial was too severe for poor humanity to sustain. As prisoner after prisoner passed on and the face of the one she sought appeared not, the light of hope began to die out of her eyes, the pallor of weariness to cover her face, and when some voice of doom called out, "This is the very last file that is passing," it was as if the waves of despair were rolling over and ingulfing her soul beneath their cruel waters, for she knew that her husband was not there.

No! no! The very last had not yet passed. It was some stolid creature, careless of the death pangs of hope in a breaking heart, that raised that false and cruel cry. The very last file had not passed. In this camp they had first inspected the records of the dead, for there the discouraged wife had feared that the name they sought would be found. How else than by his death could his long silence be explained? His name was not upon the long death-roll. They had next gone through every ward in the hospital, and as they supposed had seen every living prisoner whose name was not upon the general roster. They had not. The general who had inspected the camp had found a few tents not in use. He knew their value to save men who would die in an inclosed building. He had ordered these tents to be pitched on some elevated ground, and into them some thirty very sick men had been removed who were now convalescent.

These patients were next directed to form a line. They did so with sullen murmurings and complaints, for they with recovered health had lost the will and almost the power of physical movement. And the wife was almost compelled by Bedell to again take her place in the reviewing tent. She did it with the feeling of one compelled to reascend the scaffold because the hangman's rope had broken on the first trial. She took her seat; she awaited their coming, inanimate, hopeless almost, as themselves. The chance that her husband was among them was too slender to sustain a hope. If he was not there, what a life of desolation lay before her! If he was not there he was dead. When and where he died she was never to know. If his bones were not bleaching upon some field of death, if stranger hands had covered them with his mother earth—he had been buried in an unrecorded grave—where it was or when he died, she should never know.

She was listless and indifferent when they told her that the line was approaching. Some of those who formed it were feeble and moved very slowly, none of them with activity or animation. Bedell made one more effort to revive her spirits and rekindle her hope. It was too late. There was only one thing in the wide world that would now inspire her with the wish to live. She thanked Bedell in her heart for his kindness to her, and then she thought it pitiable that he should waste his time and energy upon one so useless as she deemed herself to be. By a last effort, as she believed it to be, of her will power, she raised her eyes high enough to scan the passing faces. One! two! three—twenty of them had passed, and there was no life in her dull eye, no expression upon her stony face. Only ten remain. More listless, cold, and hopeless than before, she for the last time turns her head and glances down the short line over its diminished numbers. But mark! why does she start as if transfixed by a bolt of lightning launched from the hand of Jove? Why does the light of life and love flame out from that weary eye? Why does that look of devout thanksgiving illuminate that stony face? See! she starts! Like a mother leaping to grasp her child saved from sudden death, she bounds from her seat. Half-way down the line she marks a well-known form. Like an arrow from the bow she clears the intervening space, she grasps with all her revived strength the poor, pale, emaciated form of one who faints in her embrace, and the palpitating heart of her husband is beating against her own.

CHAPTER XXVII.

THE HARD LOT OF A PRISONER OF WAR—ONE OF THEM TOUCHES THE END OF HIS SUFFERINGS.

Of all the miseries of war imprisonment is the chief. There is no condition of human existence so destructive to the life of the mind as well as the body as that of a prisoner of war. In all other species of confinement the man has something to which he can look forward. He knows there is to be an end to it. The term is fixed in most cases, and when it is not he can determine it proximately. In our great civil war the only certainty the prisoner had was that there was to be no exchange. Escape or the end of the war alone would give him his freedom. After a brief experience few of them had the energy for an attempt to escape, and when the end of the war would come no man could foretell.

Occupation is a necessity of human life. The mind unemployed always broods over the past. In the case of a healthy man protracted idleness inevitably causes despondency, and despondency too often death. Those who were in civil life saw the results and heard of the horrors of Andersonville and Belle Isle. But we had no conception of the dread of the soldiers for those terrible hells. Many a brave man resisted to his death rather than to go to one of those prisons and slowly perish. "Surrender, or we will bayonet you!" shouted their pursuers to the belated skirmishers leaping from tie to tie on the railroad bridge across the Monocacy, when overtaken by an overwhelming Confederate force which captured only those upon which they could lay hands. The others crossed and threw themselves into the bushes, while their bayoneted companions fell forty feet into the river, some of them to survive the battle and the war.

Van Metre had had experience in captivity for some months before his last capture. Even in Camp Chase, well known as the healthiest of the prison camps, he had become so enfeebled that he believed death was inevitable, and so took the risk of attempting to escape. At Point Lookout, confined in an unhealthy locality, guarded by negroes with whom he could have no conversation, he was very soon in a favorable condition of body for an early and a severe attack of the prevailing epidemic. Before describing his experience more minutely, it may interest the reader to make a brief reference to the effects of confinement upon the prisoners in some of the other places of detention.

In the experience of modern wars no place has

ever approached in its horrors or its mortality the prison pen of Andersonville. Its infernal destructiveness may have been chargeable to a large extent to the ferocious brute who had it under control. But its condition was not altogether unknown to the Confederate authorities, for several Southern officers of high rank repeatedly protested against the cruelty of herding so large a number of prisoners there, under conditions so fatal to human life. I am not discussing here the question of responsibility for it. It fully meets my purpose to make a statement which cannot be controverted, that every individual who was there for so long a term as three months perished if he did not make an intelligent fight for his life.

I knew a young private who had wasted over a year in that horrible den, and who after Appomattox was released in a fairly good condition of health. I asked him how he managed to preserve his life when so many stronger men perished. He appeared to make no effort to control his emotions when he replied.

"I ought," he said, "to blush with shame for my own selfishness when I answer that question. But I will try to answer it truly. When I was put inside of that stockade, all those thousands were living like burrowing animals in holes, wherever they could make an excavation. The water was foul and sickening—they could not get enough of it to wash their feet and hands once in ten days; the food was insufficient in quantity and unfit for anything living to eat; their clothes were in rags—they seemed to have lost all desire for a decent appearance. They all had that look of hopeless despondency which I never saw elsewhere. They had no exercise. You may judge how they wanted it when I assure you that men fought for the privilege of going out each morning to bury the dead and to grub the roots of stumps and dead trees for a little wood. Their deaths were frequent and often inexplicable. They died without an effort to live. Men apparently as well as the average at sunset were cold in death before the next morning.

"I had read in my boyhood of one prisoner who tamed a mouse, of another who cultivated a flower in his captivity. I knew now why they became so attached to these little objects. I knew that there was only one way for me to escape the common fate. I must keep my mind and body both employed—not an easy thing to be done where every prisoner was searched and everything taken from him. I had a plug of tobacco and an old jack-knife which I managed to secrete when I was searched upon my arrival. I cut the tobacco into small cubes, and these were my stock in trade —my capital. These I traded for bits of candle, pieces of wood, buttons, a needle and thread—for anything of which any use could be made. I am ashamed to tell you how mean and selfish I was.

Until then I never knew how contemptible a wretch I could make of myself. I haggled, lied, argued, played the tricks of the horse-jockey. I have spent an hour and got very angry over one of these trades. I have sometimes traded a poor fellow out of something useful, and then given it back to him, for it was occupation and not profit I was seeking. I soon accumulated stock and became a capitalist, for I was economical and gave my whole time to my mercantile business. What a luxury it was to me to give to some poor dying man some little delicacy which I was able to purchase for him!

"Then the villain Wurtz did me a great favor. He robbed me of all my accumulations. He made me mad up to the point of recklessness. I told him to his face that he was a brute—a merciless wretch—a cold-blooded murderer. I expected that he would draw his revolver and shoot me down. Instead of that he cringed like the coward he was. Then I told him that I should live to see him hung, and that I would be there at the entertainment if I had to walk barefooted a thousand miles. Thank God, I saw him hung! I was a witness on his trial. It was very wicked, I know, but when I saw him struggling in the agonies of death I prayed that they might be lengthened and drawn out until he paid for every one of his murders by a good half-hour of dying torture. I was a willing witness, and some of his judges said that my testimony was very convincing.

"I say he did me a favor, for when he robbed me I was at first inclined to give up and fight for life no longer. But the storm cleared my mind and made me resolve that the brute should not have the gratification of my death. I went again to my business, and I continued it until we left that dreadful place in advance of Sherman marching through Georgia. In short, by incessant occupation of body and mind I saved my own life, when thousands of better and stronger men sank under the trial and were carried to their graves."

Van Metre, when first taken prisoner, was a young man in vigorous health. He began to suffer in Camp Chase, and he was weakened by hunger and exposure in making his way on foot and in the night all that long way from Central Ohio to the army of Virginia. His experiences from his second capture have already been described. When he was discovered by the daughter of the Union general he was very near the end of his suffering and his life. In some respects his case was not unlike Bedell's, for his life had been saved by the ministrations of a woman. Her kindness and skilful nursing, her personal interest in him which again kindled hope in his heart, had literally called him back from the borders of the grave. But when she left him and went elsewhere, when day after day passed and brought no answer to his letter, no news of his wife or his home, he again gave up all hope, and lost with his strength all desire to live. He was waiting and praying for death when the hour of his delivery came.

Our heroine's long search was ended now. The true-hearted woman of the valley brought the order for his discharge at the moment when she held him in her loving arms. But her trials were not all ended. The frail, emaciated being she had found was but a poor substitute for the strong, vigorous husband she had given to the Confederacy. He could scarcely stand erect. He fainted in the joy of recognition and she carried him into the tent away from the gaze of the crowd. She laid him on his cot as tenderly as if he were her child. He soon recovered his consciousness, but a sharp pang pierced her heart when she saw his weakness and was by no means certain that he would ever be stronger.

Possibly he never would have been with ordinary treatment. Upon that treatment he was not required to depend. The time had come for Bedell to exhibit his value as a curative agent. It was appointed to him to give to the worn and weary prisoner beauty for ashes, the oil of joy for mourning, and the garment of praise for the spirit of heaviness. Minus his limb, Richard was himself again. He had recovered his splendid vigor of body and, now that Van Metre was found, his overflowing exuberance of spirits. Wherever he went he carried with him an atmosphere of invigoration, and every time he came into the sick man's presence he brought an abundant supply of courage, health, and hope.

He knew that joy never killed. He had no fear that any sick man could be made worse by the presence of Betty Van Metre. He was careful to see that she was provided with remedies and restoratives, and then he left the long-separated to their mutual and natural confidences.

But not for too long a time, for he suspected that they might devise some plans for their immediate future which would interfere with his own arrangements. Therefore, early one morning he entered their tent as he supposed in the most quiet and noiseless manner, but in fact with the roar of a small cyclone, and, in a voice ringing with cheerfulness, demanded to know whether they would be ready to leave for the Green Mountains next morning.

It was as he half supposed. As soon as Van Metre was strong enough to converse, their thoughts had turned toward their home. Van Metre knew nothing of the obligations of the Union officer to his wife, and in her joy over the recovery of her husband the arrangement made at Harper's Ferry had for the moment escaped her memory. They had agreed that it would be necessary to remain where they were until Van

Metre was strong enough to travel, when they would go to Harper's Ferry, and, as soon as they could, they would thence make their way to the homestead in Clarke County.

"I have an objection to that arrangement," said Bedell, "which makes it impossible. It ought not to be done and it cannot be done."

"I do not see why it is impossible," said Van Metre, "if, as I am informed, an order exists for my discharge."

"The reasons are so numerous that I have not counted them," was Bedell's reply. "The natural justice of your wife should have pointed out to both of you that your return to the valley, or your movement in any other direction than to my home in Vermont, cannot now be considered. In the first place, she is under contract to go there, and has already sent forward her niece as a pledge for its performance. She is too honorable to recede from a fair agreement. Then there is no place where you, Van Metre, can recover your health and spirits so quickly and so certainly as in the pure, crisp air of our Green Mountains. Berryville is now within the Confederate lines, and though Secretary Stanton has evinced his high esteem for Mrs. Van Metre, I doubt whether he would give her a pass to go there. Finally, you and I, Van Metre, have done our full share of the fighting in this war. I have left a good fourth of my body somewhere on the banks of the Opequan; you have indefinitely scattered your health between Camp Chase in Central Ohio and the James River. Now suppose we offset our remaining military value, one against the other, and let others finish the fighting of which we have done our share. Then you shall come to Vermont with me, and when your health and strength are restored we can lay plans for the future. If you could now return to the valley, they would again force you into the service."

"But why should I impose myself upon you in Vermont?" demanded Van Metre. "What have I done that you should make me a proposition so liberal?"

"You, perhaps, have done nothing. Your wife has saved my life in the hope that her doing so might benefit you. I shall leave her to give you that history. I am not the man to disappoint her hope."

"This is all new to me," protested Van Metre. "I suppose I ought to remain here for a time. I am scarcely able now to endure the fatigue of travel. When I am, I would like to do what is best and right. What that will be I do not know, for my judgment has failed with my health. I will leave the decision to my wife and to you."

"Then we may as well decide now to comply with the suggestions of the lieutenant," said Mrs. Van Metre. "His wife controls me without an effort and without resistance. He may establish a similar control over you."

"Yielding to reason is not control." said Bedell. "Men persuade, they do not control each other."

Two points upon the Potomac River should be forever noted in history for their association with the miseries of war. They are Acquia Creek, in Stafford County, about twenty miles below Washington, and Point Lookout, the peninsula formed by the junction of the Potomac River and Chesapeake Bay. The first was the place where the wounded from the terrible battles of the summer of 1864 were collected for transportation by steamer to Washington; the second, the camp where the prisoners from the same battles were confined. Twenty thousand wounded men have been collected at Acquia Creek from the conflicts of a single week. Twenty thousand prisoners have been confined at Point Lookout at one time. That number of idle men anywhere would breed discomfort and disease, but at Point Lookout there were special facilities for misery. There were dense, damp winter fogs that pierced to the very marrow; there were no facilities for heating and the sick in the hospitals were among the chief sufferers. Van Metre insisted upon the constant presence of Bedell in his tent, for he said his face was a better preventive than quinine for the chills which followed his fever and were increased in length and discomfort by the gloomy weather. Bedell endured this discomfort only for a few days. A morning came when he took command of the situation. Entering the tent where Mrs. Van Metre was vainly endeavoring to extract the cold and moisture from the atmosphere by a liberal combustion of kerosene, he exclaimed:

"Come! Make such preparations as you can to leave this dismal place. I have provided for the safety and comfort of the patient. As soon as you can get ready, a steamer will leave this camp for Washington with no passengers but ourselves. We are to have the use of the well-heated ladies' cabin. We will start for a country where the atmosphere is suited to honest men and good women. Here a little air makes one wish to die; there, the more of it you breathe the more you wish to live. Van Metre," he said, warming with enthusiasm, "if at this moment you were sitting before my big fireplace, with the chimney roaring like the escaping steam in a locomotive as the flames go up from the maple back-log, with the children cracking butternuts on the hearth, a pitcher of cider on the table, and your wife with a happy face sewing by your side, the winds and the weather might rage like the heathen out-of-doors and they would not disturb you. That country is white and cold in winter out-of-doors, but the hearts and the homes of its people are warm at all seasons. For that country we start this morning."

"We cannot! We have talked the matter over and it would not be right to burden——"

"Not another word! I am the stronger now and I am going to take command and charge, just as you did when I lay helpless in that desolate room. You, madam, have only yourself to prepare. The nurses will carry your husband on board. If you make any resistance they will also carry you. I see they are coming now."

Mrs. Van Metre surrendered. She had no power to withstand such impetuosity. Besides, in her heart she believed that the change and the company of Bedell would lift her husband out of his present depression and restore him to health. Her preparations therefore involved no delay. Under the Secretary's order she receipted for the body of her husband; he was carried on board with the crippled officer and herself as his only companions; the lines of the steamer were cast off, and as she gracefully swept around the first turn in the river Point Lookout forever disappeared from their view.

The condition of Van Metre improved with every mile left astern by the steamer. By the time they reached the landing in Washington, he was moving about the cabin slightly assisted by his wife. The steamer was to lie at her wharf for some repairs to her machinery. The whole party lived quietly on board, Bedell only leaving her long enough to arrange for their transportation to Vermont and to discharge a most agreeable duty. He called upon General Hitchcock and Secretary Stanton and informed them of the success of the search for Van Metre. He learned that justice did not travel with leaden feet in the War Department. The report of the veteran inspector of prisons had produced an order for a court-martial to try the faithless wretch who had brought Van Metre so near to the gates of death. But for a providential favor he would have been recalled from Vermont as a witness upon the trial. But the culprit met his deserts in a more speedy way. He learned of the order for his trial on the day that the party left the camp. He stole a small boat and started to cross the river, preferring to take his chances with the Confederates. He was discovered and ordered by the sentinel to return. He disobeyed the order and kept on his way; but he could not outspeed the bullet from the Winchester which sped through his merciless heart. He plunged overboard and disappeared beneath the muddy waters of the Potomac. It was a more merciful death than he deserved, and it anticipated only by a few days his execution by the sentence of a court-martial. For just then the people of the North were beginning to appreciate how great a volume of human suffering could be created by one such man in a camp of prisoners of war, and were demanding, in tones that struck terror to the hearts of incompetent or faithless officers, kind and considerate treatment for the captured.

CHAPTER XXVIII.

"WEEPING MAY ENDURE FOR A NIGHT, BUT JOY COMETH IN THE MORNING."

FROM the miseries of the prison camp, the thunder of battle, and the turmoil of bloody war, we turn to the peace and quiet of the north country. Nature has just prepared it for a festival of thanksgiving. Through the night the snow-flakes with noiseless wing have been covering the earth with a garment of spotless purity. Just when it was finishing, a gentle warmth has molded these flakes into crystals which have converted every naked branch into a drooping spray, heavy with jewels which glint and sparkle like diamonds in the yellow rays of the morning sun. Nature loves contrasts, and lovely as emeralds in their silver settings are the dark evergreens above the snow. The air is cold, but it teems with electric life. The horses are sportive in harness, the cattle and the sheep are leaping and racing in the farm-yards—animal nature is full to the overflow of vivacity and exhilaration.

There is no wind. The blue smoke from the early-lighted hearths of the scattered homes goes straight upward until it is lost in the air filled with innumerable scales of frozen moisture. With ruddy faces and frosted breath, the sturdy farmers turn out with their spirited but well-broken teams to break out the roads and tread the snow so that their polished sleigh-runners shall draw musical sounds from the cold, hard path over which they swiftly glide. If on the face of the earth there is a region where man with every breath draws in a new supply of health and strength and glorious vigor of body and mind, it is Vermont on a winter's morning.

There is one household in which unusual activity prevails. From early dawn its mistress with her own family and a young girl visitor have been busy in preparation and decoration. In the kitchen she has been the Lady Bountiful, and now they are making the house beautiful with wreaths of evergreens. Opposite the front door, along the walls of the square room, in large capitals out of the branches of the hemlock and the cedar are formed the words "Welcome home." Many times during the day a neighbor's team has dashed up to the door, and an eager face thrust inside has asked, "Are you certain they are coming to-night?" And every one has had the same answer, "Yes! certain. We have telegrams from them; we know that they are on the train."

There are hearts in that household whose loving impatience is too powerful to be suppressed. As often as once every half-hour the temporary master of the household, the little colonel, has had to be assured that the clock has not stopped. When it has been opened to show him the pendulum still swinging, he has declared that he had doubted the statement in the Sunday-school lesson that "the sun stood still upon Gibeon," but there was no doubt whatever that to-day it stood still upon Jay Mountain. The test of his self-restraint was still more severe when toward evening he saw the sleighs of the neighbors moving swiftly toward the railroad station and he knew that others would welcome his brave father before he saw the face of his own son. With the approach of darkness he was given employment. He had lighted the lamps and placed them in the windows, so many and so bright that from a distance the whole house seemed ablaze.

Then they all waited for the promised signal from the railway station, doubtful whether it could be heard so far. But fortune had suspended its persecutions for the time, and the hand of the clock moved never so slowly, but was coming very near to the time when the train would be due. One more minute passes. This time the locomotive will not disappoint them. It seems to feel the strong attraction of loving hearts for each other and shows its best speed. With a fierce triumphant scream, it hauls the train into the station two whole minutes ahead of time.

At the moment of the whistle a torrent of flame bursts from the muzzle of the borrowed cannon, spreads outward and upward like a sea wave, and recoils from the rock faces of the mountain. Do they hear it in the home of the Bedells? They could not close their impatient ears against it, for now every rock that responds to the discharges in quick succession unites them into a thunder roll heard through all the region, as if mountain, forest, and tree were breaking forth into rejoicings to welcome a brave soldier returning from the wars.

And now the moment has come for which the boy and his comrades have waited so impatiently. They have prepared their own signal of welcome. It is on an elevation; away from the buildings they have set up a huge pile of dry logs on end. To-day they have swept away every flake of snow and filled the interstices with splinters of fat pine. Each boy now seizes his lighted torch and fires the pile all around the base. The flames creep swiftly around every log, then leap to the summit, and a circular pyramid of fire lights up the road to the station and illuminates the surrounding country.

The cheers of many voices succeed to the reports of cannon. Over a distant hill comes a team. Its four spirited horses scatter music from their bells as, under the guiding reins of their skilful driver, they speed along the snowy road as if proud of the burden they draw. Fearless of the bonfire, never once breaking their swift trotting step, they dash up to and stand like statues before an open door. Something large and very much alive within an army overcoat springs from the sleigh on a single leg and with both arms grasps a woman who fears the giant embrace so little that she does not turn away her face. There is a creaking, osculatory sound as when the sleigh moves swiftly over the cold, hard snow. Then the arm of the overcoat lifts a man out of the conveyance and sets him on his feet. A woman follows—the two women meet with more sounds of osculation. An irregular procession, with a cripple using his wife as a substitute for a lacking leg and with children swarming up his back, at its head, enters the house, followed by two strangers, and the Van Metres are within the hospitable home of the Bedells.

The travellers have reached a haven where there is no anxiety or fear. The guests are extracted from their unaccustomed polar wraps and shown to a room on the ground-floor, with a warning that but little time can be spared them for preparation, for a slight repast is waiting which must be cleared away before the fast teams of the neighbors who met them at the station can gather in their wives and daughters and return. They conformed to the wishes of their hostess and were soon seated at her board of simple New England fare. She was unable to set before them anything more appetizing than a young turkey, with its chestnut stuffing and cranberry accessories, young and tender chickens roasted, fricasseed, broiled, and browned into a pie with flaky crust, a boiled ham of a delicate pink color, sausages, apple-sauce with boiled cider, and a miscellaneous assortment of puddings, mince, apple, custard, and golden pumpkin pies serving as side-dishes and dessert. With these and other incidentals the travellers managed to keep hunger at a distance for the time. They had scarcely done justice to the homely cheer before the music of the sleigh-bells and the runners creaking upon the hard snow announced the coming of the guests. The "welcome" on the wall pervaded the house. Never, even in warm-hearted Vermont, was it more cordial than that of his fellow-citizens and their wives to Bedell and to the woman who had saved his life; never was it more warmly reciprocated than by Bedell and his efficient wife.

The Van Metres would have appropriated none of this cordiality to themselves, and yet they could not but feel more like honored guests than strangers. Van Metre had borne the journey well. He was stronger than when he left Washington. But Bedell would take no risks, and after he was presented to the guests insisted that he should retire. The bed was so much more comfortable than any which he had used since his first capture that it was a long time before he could compose himself to sleep.

For the absence of the heroine of the valley the guests would accept no excuse. She was the attraction of the evening—the brave woman who had saved the life of their fellow-citizen. She it was whom the husbands came to honor, their wives to know and to love.

That was also a memorable occasion for Bedell. He learned how well he stood in the esteem of his neighbors, and he was not spoiled by their praises. He could not decline to gratify their desire to hear an account of his life in the valley, though his story was little more than a hymn of praises for his preserver. She, poor woman, was as much embarrassed as she had been in the presence of Secretary Stanton. She had a hard experience with the impetuous beings of her own sex. After her husband retired, Mrs. Bedell took her arm and with it exclusive possession of her person. She presented her to the wives of her neighbors as her creditor for her husband's life. She extolled her courage and her fearless performance of her duty. "She is henceforth to be my sister," she said, "with whom I hope to share whatever of good fortune hereafter comes to me."

The modest Virginian, so fearless in the presence of real danger, was overcome by the love of many generous hearts. She appealed to her hostess with the simplicity of a child. "You must assist me," she said. "I cannot think what I ought to say—the words will not come. I must be losing the little mind I once possessed; if you do not help me they will think me very stupid!"

"Then do not try to think or speak," was the counsel of her friend. "You are with those who will appreciate your silence far better than my volubility."

She did break the silence, however, when, as she claimed, Bedell was giving her a credit to which she thought she was not entitled. She cautioned his neighbors against believing all his statements about herself, for, said she a little mischievously, "he was not always himself in those trying days, and some of his impressions may have been caused by his delirium." But her protestations could not suppress the essential facts. She had found Bedell in the very grasp of death. She had saved him. But for her his body would now have been buried in the distant region where he had left his amputated limb. Through her, he was now surrounded by his family and friends with a prospect before him of a long and useful life. Such an undisputed service was enough to give her a warm place in their hearts and an esteem which they knew how to express without annoyance to a modest woman. They showed their consideration in many ways. They knew the day had been a weary one for her, and that the family of Bedell were entitled to his undisturbed possession. As soon as they had shown to Mrs. Van Metre how thoroughly her conduct was appreciated, how welcome she was in the community to which she had returned a valued citizen, and to Bedell how well he stood in their esteem, the guests withdrew. But there was no man or woman of them who did not bestow upon her a parting benediction which made her grateful that without fear of consequences or the censorship of man she had done her duty.

There are none of the promises of Scripture more precious than those of rest to the weary soul. There was never a weary heart to whom rest was more grateful than that of the woman whose life for less than a half-year we have attempted to describe. For almost four years she had endured the privations and miseries of war. Every hour of her life had been broken by anxiety and distress. She had been reduced to poverty, her nerves had been shattered by the roar of battle, her heart pierced by the sufferings of the wounded, her eyes dimmed by pictures of the dying; she had mourned her husband as among the dead. In all these years when there was not a gleam of light, not a rift in the dark horizon of her life, she had never yielded. She had always bravely met her apparent duty. Now, at last, she was in the quiet of the country, surrounded by friends where there was none to molest or make her afraid. Her husband was with her;

he might recover and have a long and useful life. Now she knew the meaning of the promise, "Ye shall find rest unto your souls."

Van Metre also had suffered. He had loyally served under his flag, he had endured all that man could endure and live. With him days had grown into weeks and weeks into months of suffering more acute than death on the field. If now when enfeebled by disease he decided not to return to the service, no man could justly charge him with any failure to perform his duty.

As the winter passed and the Union lines, stronger in number of their defenders, were contracting around Richmond, and it was apparent that the end of the war was approaching, by the inevitable result of all future wars between nations of Saxon origin, the exhaustion of the weaker party, Bedell and Van Metre felt no desire to fight their battles over again, and were quite content to be spectators of the closing struggle.

The time had come when the modest, brave woman of the valley was beginning to enjoy the reward of her heroic performance of her woman's duty. There was a marvellous change in her appearance. The weary movement of her body disappeared; the color of health upon her face was fixed; the sad expression of her eyes was replaced by the light of joy and hope. Her step became elastic, her figure lithe and graceful. She became an universal favorite, especially with the young. She entered into their plans and plays with the spirit of a young girl. She was quick to relieve her hostess of the service of the household on the plea that she was a learner of New England ways. She travelled miles to nurse the sick and comfort the mourner, because, as she maintained, she must have the exercise. Her sweet nature expanded and grew more attractive under New England culture until it reached its matured perfection.

Time waits neither for a Vermont nor a Virginia farmer. There was no complaint about his slowness now. The members of this household had been so happy in the society of each other that before they were conscious how time was passing, winter was reposing in the lap of spring. Bedell, grown strong and stalwart, was now unfitted by his loss for a farmer's life, and must accept or decline an advantageous offer to exchange his farm for an established business in a neighboring town. Van Metre felt that he had tarried at Westfield until his beard was grown. It was heavier now than the one he lost at Point Lookout. His face had lost its pallor, his muscles had recovered their former density. Sheridan had harrowed the valley for the last time. If the valley farm was to be made as attractive and productive as before it was blasted by the hot breath of war, its owner must go back and prepare it for the planting and sowing of the spring.

And so with one more separation, the relations of the Bedells and the Van Metres are brought to an end. This young Virginia woman, unconsciously and without an effort, has set before the world an example which ought to make her name a household word in the Republic. The soldier whose life she saved has repaid a part of his debt by the restoration of her husband. He now bids her farewell, but he will carry to his grave the memory of his preserver, the true woman and the unconscious heroine.

NOTE.

This volume is illustrated by portraits of Mrs. Van Metre and Lieutenant Bedell. Their portraits would have been more satisfactory if they had represented their respective originals at the time when the events occurred which are here recorded. But no photographs of either of so early a date existed. Those from which these portraits are drawn were taken, that of Mrs. Van Meter about twelve and of Mr. Bedell about fifteen years after the close of the war. Both represent characters capable of the acts attributed to them.

No effort has been made to trace the descent of either of the principal characters in this book to any distinguished ancestry. But they are all of good blood. A very casual acquaintance with the history of the Shenandoah Valley settles the question as to the Keysers and the Van Metres. Very early in the history of the valley there was an emigration to it of Hollanders and Germans from New York and Pennsylvania.

The limestone lands about the headwaters of the Opequan Creek were attractive to them. The town of Woodstock was exclusively settled by them, and for many years the Dutch and German languages were the only ones spoken in that settlement. Dutch customs have survived there to the present time. These settlers were among the sturdy patriots of the Revolution. It was in the town of Woodstock that Maj.-Gen. John Peter Gabriel Muhlenberg, minister of the Lutheran Church, dressed in his uniform, with his sword buckled to his side, preached a farewell sermon, in 1776, to his patriotic congregation, and the next day marched as colonel at the head of his regiment to join the Continental army. Such names as Strasburg, Mecklenberg, Hamburg, and others show that many of the early settlers of the section were of German origin.

Among these early settlers were the Van Metres and the Keysers. Washington's journal, kept while he was surveying the lands of Lord Fairfax, in the valley, under date of March 27th, 1748, records that he "Travell'd over to ye South Branch attended with ye Esqr. to Henry Van Metre's, in order to go about intended work of lots." The Van Metres were a numerous family and among the earliest settlers in the valley, on the South Branch and along the Upper Potomac. Kercheval in his history says they were people of energy and good judges of land. John Van Metre was an Indian trader, who accompanied the Delaware Indians in a war party against the Catawbas, but the Catawbas, anticipating the attack, surprised and defeated the Delawares in a battle near where the courthouse of Pendleton now stands. John Van Metre escaped and returned to New York, but he was so impressed with the beauty and fertility of the lands on the South Branch bottom, in Hardy County, that he advised his sons to secure lands and locate there. Of these sons, Isaac became a man of note and frequently represented Hardy County in the House of Delegates of Virginia. He was a member of the Virginia Convention of 1788, which ratified the Federal Constitution. In 1730 it is a matter of history that John and Isaac Van Metre, brothers, obtained from Governor Gooch, of Virginia, a warrant for 40,000 acres of land, to be located west of the mountains. This warrant, or a part of it, they sold to Joost Hite.

A number of tracts on the original warrant were surveyed in the vicinity of Shepherdstown. The name of Van Metre is still frequently met with throughout West Virginia, and has its monument in a stream forming the northwestern boundary line of Jefferson County and emptying into the Potomac, and named on the maps of Virginia Van Metre's Marsh. A controversy as to the validity of the Van Metre patent was raised in 1738 by Lord Fairfax and taken into the courts for adjudication, Lord Fairfax contending that his grants covered the whole of the western end of the northern neck, while the holders claimed that the governor, under authority of the crown, had disposing power. This conflict as to title was a source of much litigation and was not finally settled until after the Revolution, when all the parties to the original suits were dead. (Kercheval, "History of the Valley.")

The Van Metres, like the Lincolns, were of the sterling, brave, and enterprising men who pushed across the mountains and won Kentucky and other States of the Great West from the Indians. In the second volume of that delightful book by Theodore Roosevelt, "The Winning of the West," at p. 101, I find the statement that in the spring of 1780 a congregation of the Low Dutch Reformed Church, to the number of one hundred and fifty heads of families, with their wives and children, their beasts of burden, and their household goods, came from Virginia to settle in Kentucky. In the appendix to the same volume is given a manuscript petition, now in the State Department, dated in May, 1780, stating that the settlers "are greatly exposed to the saviges by whome our wives and childring are daly cruily murdered," and praying the Continental Congress to "take proper methods to form us into a seperate state." Among the 640 signers to this petition was Abraham Van Metre.

I do not pursue the genealogy of the characters in this book, for I think they are able to stand upon their own merits. I have written this note because the facts came to my knowledge by pure accident, and it is always pleasant to know that the present generation sustains the reputation of its sturdy ancestry.

THE END.

Personal Reminiscences

1840–1890

BY

L. E. CHITTENDEN

Register of the Treasury under President Lincoln. Author of "An Unknown Heroine," etc., etc.

Large 12mo, Cloth, Gilt Top, Portrait of the Author, Price $2.00

Mr. Chittenden's career belongs in so large a measure to the history of the United States during the past fifty years, his experiences have been so varied and interesting, and his associations so memorable that this volume of his "Personal Reminiscences from 1840 to 1890" must take rank with the most noteworthy of its class, second to the great biographies, but contributing important data for the student of our social and political history. It ranges from the author's early professional life in Vermont to the mining camps in the far West, and embraces a wide range of life full of incident and graphic descriptions.

The most important section is doubtless that devoted to Mr. Lincoln and his times, and the "Study" with which the book closes . . . is a sketch by one who was intimately associated with the great Emancipator that deserves to be included with the contemporary records of the greatest character of our times.—*The Bookbuyer*, New York.

Sold by all booksellers, or sent postpaid on receipt of price by the publishers,

RICHMOND, CROSCUP & CO.

9 East 17th Street, New York

EXTRACTS FROM PRESS NOTICES.

The New York Times.

The wide range of the reminiscences is not more remarkable than their brightness and originality.

The New York Recorder.

One of the makers of history, the Hon. L. E. Chittenden, worthy descendant of the family that gave to Vermont its revolutionary governor, has added to the literature of his country a contribution of considerable value in his "Personal Reminiscences." The book is pervaded throughout by that charm which attaches to the unstudied words of one who has lived long among stirring scenes, seen shrewdly, and remembered well.

The Nation, New York.

Mr. Chittenden's reminiscences will be attractive to men of very different classes. What we have said will satisfy the book-hunter that the book is a revelation after his own heart.

Literary World, Boston.

Its fervent patriotism and loyalty to the national idols and ideas and its unobtrusive but uncompromising Christian faith and spirit make it a thoroughly quickening book to one's patriotism and religion.

Boston Traveller.

The thousands of readers of Hon. L. E. Chittenden's "Recollections of President Lincoln" will eagerly read the volume of "Personal Reminiscences" from his pen. . . . His study of Lincoln which constitutes the closing chapters is one of remarkable power of analysis and abounds in incident hitherto unpublished.

Portland Transcript.

The book is a series of delightful talk from a man of wide experience. . . . We have nothing but commendation for this book.

Baltimore Sun.

It is full of good matter of the most diverse kind, the striking recollections of an old man, a natural politician, a book-lover, a lawyer of the "forties."

Philadelphia Times.

A new book from the pen of Mr. Chittenden cannot fail to attract public interest. His story of Secretary Chase and his financial policy may be accepted as the most reliable we have from any source.

Philadelphia Inquirer.

The whole makes a most entertaining record of a well-rounded and useful life.

Chicago Times.

Mr. Chittenden makes effective reply to the old speculations as to Lincoln's religious views. The book throughout is charmingly written.

The Outlook, New York.

The last fourth of the volume is taken up with a "study" of Abraham Lincoln which will set to rest forever . . . the old questioning about Mr. Lincoln's religious faith and hope.

Boston Journal.

Future historians will find much interesting material in these personal recollections.

The New York Herald.

Mr. Chittenden's book is a valuable contribution to the literature of reminiscences.

St. Paul Dispatch.

The stories are told without literary artifice or mannerisms, and we see in it that much amusement can be taken out of the serious work of life.

Pittsburg Times.

Mr. Chittenden writes out of a full life, rich in experiences, and with accurate knowledge of human nature.

The New York World.

Mr. Chittenden has told his story so well that it has much of the incident and connection of a novel.

The Christian at Work, New York.

American literature will be the richer for this new addition to its stores.

The Beacon, Boston.

It is a volume that should have a place in every representative American library.

Burlington Free Press.

No one who takes up this book will quickly lay it down or leave many pages unread.

Toledo Bee.

Mr. Chittenden as a story-teller has few equals.

Union and Advertiser, Rochester.

It is rich in anecdote and delightfully written.

Minneapolis Tribune.

The student of history, lover of biography and of good reading should not neglect Mr. Chittenden's book.

www.ingramcontent.com/pod-product-compliance
Lightning Source LLC
Chambersburg PA
CBHW030744230426
43667CB00007B/841